MODERN

A contemporary guide to quilting by hand

QUILTING

MODERN

A contemporary guide to quilting by hand

QUILTING

JULIUS ARTHUR *of* **HOUSE OF QUINN**

PHOTOGRAPHY BY MATT RUSSELL

Hardie Grant

BOOKS

Contents

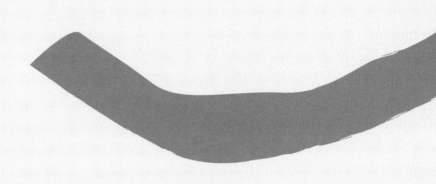

Workshops

24

Projects

72

INTRODUCTION

'For me, a quilt is about home, daily life, where you've been
and who you've known.'

Walking along the river beaches of the Fal Estuary in Cornwall, small yellow shells glinted in the afternoon sun, hidden amongst the slate grey shingle and seaweed that was scattered across the shoreline. As children, my sister and I would spend afternoons eagerly combing the beaches for the best specimens, filling our pockets as we went up and down the pebbles. Proud of our efforts and tired from our long days of foraging, we would return home to admire our finds, tipping them out across the kitchen table, and offering the gem-like yellow shells to our mother who added them to her growing collection.

Looking back on that memory, our house was always full of found objects, from gnarled wooden sticks gathered while walking in the woods, to intriguing stones or beautiful coloured pieces of glass sculpted by the sea. Dotted around the house you would also come across objects that had been passed down from family or gifted by friends. Pieces of rock crystal sat on the windowsill, bouncing light across the room; boxes of vinyl records once loved and played on the turntable were stacked up in the corner. The objects around our house weren't always of antique value or priceless family heirlooms – in fact they could be quite ordinary, utilitarian items you may expect to find in any home, but because of their attachment to a person, time or place they were loved nonetheless, each piece with its own story to tell.

The little yellow shells eventually found their place, arranged in intricate patterns across the surface of an old wooden box found in a charity shop. The newly made shell trinket box became a memento of the times we spent as children wandering the riverbanks with our parents; from finding the shells to the process of decorating the box with them, a memory of the past comes to life.

I began House of Quinn in 2016 as a design practice and a place for exploration in craft and design. Within my work I try to tell stories or encapsulate memories – stories that are often related to quiet, domestic moments or seemingly insignificant recollections of childhood. In my craft practice, I return again and again to the quilt as a conduit for those memories, which are conveyed through form, materials, colour and stitching.

For me, a quilt is about home and daily life: where you've been and who you've known. A quilt is imbued with the power to rediscover memories, open up conversations and bring people together. Much like the yellow shell box that now sits in my childhood home in Cornwall, a quilt can ground you by providing a sense of belonging.

I have always had an affinity with textiles and enjoy working with fabrics. I first experienced the joys of making as a child, before working in a fabric shop in my hometown growing up, and then moving to Sussex to attend university where I graduated in Fashion Design. Textiles have always been central to my creative outlook, and they are integral to our everyday lives.

As a resource we take fabric for granted and it is easy to forget, or not even consider, the journey a material has taken before it ends up with us. Passing through many hands, as fibres turn to cloth and cloth into 'things', the life of fabric has a story all of its own. When working with textiles, and considering their journey, I think it is important to make materials last and to respect the relationships that we have with them. Traditionally a quilt was an object made from patches of thrifted cloth stitched together by hand (see more information on pages 11–12). Over time fabrics soften and fade with age, adding character and personality. If a hole appears, it can simply be mended with a patch of something else, building up the layers as it evolves with use. Quilts are made to last and by reusing and renewing fabrics to create beautiful quilts, we can enjoy these items for a long time.

I hope that by writing this book, I can share with you some of the things I have learnt along the way and inspire you to think about having a go at renewing loved textiles into beautiful objects that will stand the test of time.

Quilts are simple luxuries for the everyday.

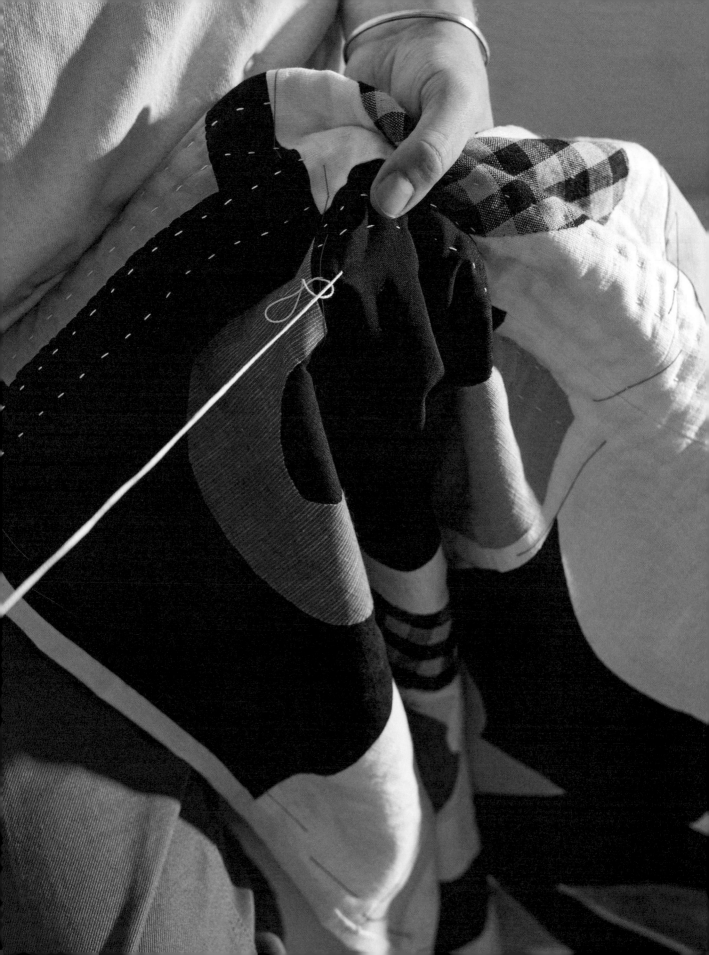

Quilting traditions

The quilt as an object has been, and still is, central to communities and cultures all around the world. Born from practical necessity, quilts also have the ability to tell stories. The rich and diverse history of quilting, and the communities that stitched them by hand, have inspired many aspects of modern quilting, from using traditional sewing techniques to communicating a narrative. Predominantly it has been the women of each community who have made quilts, often as an outlet to express their innate creativity. We have these people to acknowledge for sharing their stories and passing down the skills that they have honed over time.

In writing this book I have used the term 'informal quilting' as a way to bring together various quilting methods that I use in my work; it's a merger between traditional piecing, improvisational quilting and appliqué processes. The techniques used in this book can be found in many quilting traditions around the world. To talk about quilting and share the skills I have learnt would not be possible without the makers who came before, who paved the way for modern quilting.

The making of wholecloth and strippy quilts was a traditional skill passed down through generations in the northeast of England, Wales and the Scottish borders. The quilt top is a single piece of fabric, or made in simple wide strips, so the beauty of the quilt lies in its complex stitching patterns. In the 19th and early 20th centuries, professional quilters would travel around making quilts to order, and each area developed its own regional style and popular motifs.

In North America, quiltmakers increasingly created quilt blocks that could be sewn together into the quilt top, as blocks were small and more easily portable for settlers on the move. The lack of large pieces of cloth also meant that quilters had to use smaller pieces left over or salvaged from other items. Some of the most well-known examples of American quilting come from the Amish, self-contained communities who live simple lives. Made from fabric left over from garment making, Amish quilts usually feature rich jewel-like colours and bold geometric shapes.

Improvisational quilting, which takes a more abstract and free-form approach to quiltmaking, has its roots in African and African-American quilting. The most well-known examples were – and still are – made by the Gee's Bend quilters of Alabama. The Gee's Bend was a cotton plantation and quilts were made by slaves, who in the 18th and 19th centuries used clothes and cotton sacks to create quilts to keep themselves and their families warm. These quilts have become some of the most influential examples of quilt design and a reminder of the importance of the quilt in African-American communities.

The Kantha quilts of Bangladesh and Bengal are traditionally made from saris layered and stitched to create the bedspreads and quilts used in the home. Usually sewn by women, these quilts are not only beautiful in their appearance and process, but are a significant part of traditional life in these regions, using the materials at hand to create work that provides income, comfort and represents the rich history and stories of the women who made them.

Boro mending and sashiko stitching originated in Japan, where in farming and rural regions textiles were precious and it was more economical to reuse cloth than to purchase new. Boro is the process in which clothes and fabrics are patchworked, mended and stitched to expand their use. Sashiko features closely-spaced lines of decorative and precise stitching, creating intricate patterns that run along the surface of the textiles reinforcing and extending their longevity and practical application.

Quilts have also been part of the fight for change, equality and remembrance. In 1987 the AIDS Memorial Quilt was first displayed in Washington DC. One of the world's largest community craft projects to this day, this quilt was created by thousands to honour, remember and celebrate those who lost their lives or were affected by the HIV-AIDS pandemic. It is a quilt that fought for change and raised awareness for communities who were not given the same rights as others. The quilt was conceived by gay rights activist Cleve Jones and stands as a reminder of progress for LGBTQIA+ communities around the world.

To acknowledge quilting's rich past is to understand that quilts will remain important in our future. I have mentioned here only a few major traditions in quilting's long and diverse history that have had a particular influence on my work. As we learn and develop from each other we must celebrate, remember and appreciate the traditions of others, acknowledging their stories and history. My aim in writing this book is to provide you with creative ways to express yourself and create visual stories through experimenting and making with textiles. But as we all learn from each other, I hope you will also find ways to discover the narratives of others along the way: to learn from each other is to better understand one another, no matter where we come from or who we are.

In dedication to those who quilted before.

How to use this book

Combining a traditional craft with a contemporary application of shape and colour, *Modern Quilting* teaches you how to master the basic quilting stitches and techniques and apply them to a series of 20 creative projects. With a focus on hand stitching, this book encourages you to experiment with textiles to create meaningful items for your living spaces, places and daily rituals.

WORKSHOPS

Making quilts is a creative process but its foundations are built around a series of core techniques. In this book you will find four workshop chapters to guide you through the fundamentals of quiltmaking. These workshops are broken down into simple step-by-step instructions, accompanied by illustrated guides and photos to help you learn and also to inspire you. You can refer back to these techniques when making any of the projects in the book.

PROJECTS

Inspired by memories from my childhood and items I love to make in the studio, you will find a series of quilts and other items, such as cushions, bags and wallhangings, you can make from patchwork, appliqué and stitched textiles to bring your newfound skills to life. Each project has a series of step-by-step instructions to help you. I have also included recommendations for fabric types and colours but I encourage you to experiment with colour palettes and textiles that resonate with you.

TEMPLATES

Templates are used throughout the book to help you cut your fabric to the correct measurements and act as a placement guide. Instructions on how to make them are provided in each relevant project. These templates can be made from thick paper or thin card that can easily be found around the house and can be a great way to recycle these materials into something useful to use in your projects. If you want to make more than one of the same item, you can reuse your template over and over again.

Tools and equipment

Quilts can be made with a collection of simple tools and equipment that are easy to source or that you may already have at home. I have provided a list of items that I use on a regular basis when making quilts. Over time you will learn which tools suit your needs and way of working, so I advise you to experiment and find the pieces of kit that work best for you.

Scissors – Sharp fabric scissors, with a 20-cm (8-in) blade or smaller, are a quilter's best friend (along with the rotary cutter). Find a good pair that suit you and they will serve you well when making quilts.

Thread snips – Small scissors or snips are used for detailed work or snipping threads close to the fabric.

Rotary cutter – A rotary cutter is used to trim quilt blocks and cut straight edges all around a quilt. It will easily become the most used tool in your kit, so I recommend treating yourself to one. I use a 4.5-cm (1¾-in) rotary cutter for most of my work. Be sure to purchase a few extra blades as they become blunt after repeated use.

Cutting mat – A cutting mat is a handy surface to cut on when using a rotary cutter and quilter's rule or straight edge. I use an A1 cutting mat but other sizes are available.

Quilter's rule and straight edge – A quilter's rule and a straight edge are both key tools for quiltmaking. I recommend using a clear acrylic quilter's rule measuring 12.5 x 58.5 cm (5 x 23 in) – they are available in either metric or imperial units. A metre rule (or yardstick) is handy when sewing larger projects.

Sewing needles – Alongside general sewing needles, hand-sewing needles are essential when working quilting stitches by hand. For quilting, I recommend a long, sharp needle with a large eye: sashiko needles or long darning needles work well. For general stitching, a mixed pack of long darning needles in sizes No.3–9 will provide you with all the needles needed for hand quilting, stitching appliqué and applying binding.

Thimbles – Over prolonged periods, quilting can be taxing on your fingers and hands. Thimbles will help protect your fingers when sewing. I recommend trying thimbles of various sizes and made from different materials until you find the right ones for you.

Quilter's crease/Hera marker – A tool used to mark fabric temporarily by creasing a line in the cloth. It comes in one size and can be found in most haberdasheries or sewing stores.

Tailor's chalk – I prefer to use white chalk as coloured chalk can stain some fabrics. Light chalk marks can be removed with a stiff brush or will come out when washed.

Fabric markers – There are many types of fabric markers available, but my advice before using one is to test it on a fabric scrap first. Markers can react differently when subjected to heat or washing so always test each one before using on your quilt tops.

Masking tape – Low-tack masking tape is used to mark stitching guides when quilting, stabilising backing fabric when constructing, removing lint and sticking templates together. Painter's tape also works well.

Sewing pins – Dressmaking pins and quilter's safety pins always come in handy. Quilter's safety pins are gently curved to pass easily through the layers of a quilt and hold them together. Dressmaking pins are used in general sewing tasks when quiltmaking.

Quilting thread – Hand quilting thread is a smooth cotton thread treated with wax to ensure that it glides easily through the layer of a quilt when used to stitch them together. You can use topstitching thread, which is slightly thicker than regular sewing thread, or embroidery thread of sashiko thread, which is made of matt cotton with a light twist. I like to use a cotton pearl crochet thread in a medium weight, or size 8. This is a thick thread that gives definition to your stitching while adding a decorative element.

Sewing thread – Good-quality sewing thread is really important when sewing patchwork, attaching binding and hand stitching appliqué. A strong, all-purpose sewing thread in cotton or polyester is best for making quilts.

Beeswax – Running your hand sewing thread over a block of tailor's beeswax a few times strengthens and smooths the thread, keeping it from tangling and knotting. Seal the beeswax into the thread by running a moderately hot iron over it, but place a scrap of fabric between the thread and iron to protect the plate.

Sewing machine – A sewing machine is very handy when making quilts. All the quilts in this book are hand quilted and hand-finished, but I have used a sewing machine to sew patchwork, attach binding and construct some of the projects in this book. However, there are ways to bind and finish a quilt without a sewing machine and there are ways around making quilts if you don't have one.

Iron and ironing board – An iron and heat-proof surface to iron on are essential for quiltmaking and appliqué.

Freezer paper – Freezer paper is a waxed paper that can be found in most haberdasheries or online. Used to make appliqué templates, this paper can be temporarily fixed to fabric with an iron.

Paper and card – Some projects in this book require templates made from thick paper or thin card. In the studio, I use dot and cross pattern cutting paper, but you can use anything from brown paper to everyday paper stuck together with masking tape.

Fabrics and textiles

Textiles often become a memento of a different time: from vintage cotton dresses worn and loved year on year, to beautiful French linen tablecloths that might have been used in gatherings with loved ones. Even newly-made fabrics have a story of their own, starting life as a plant and moving through many processes and hands until becoming a beautiful fabric. Textiles are woven into all of our lives in some way or another and I believe we should respect and consider the journey they have taken to get to us.

Fabric – For the projects that follow, I have used natural cottons and linens, which are easy to come by and perfect for quilting. It is best to find textiles that are woven, with no stretch and a light to midweight handle. Cottons and linens are also very easy to dye or decorate with paints and inks. Lighter fabrics can be dyed with tea or coffee, or by using other plant-based natural dyes, such as avocado pits. I like to use a lot of reclaimed or end-of-roll fabrics as well as fabric remnants, which you can find in most charity shops, vintage stores and antique fairs. Another great source of sustainable fabrics are clothing and household items, such as linen tablecloths or cotton curtains.

When purchasing new fabrics, consider where they come from. I don't want to put you off buying new textiles, but if you do, take some time to think about the environmental impact and what you can do to reuse and recycle where possible.

Wadding or batting – Wadding or batting refers to the soft, warm layer that makes up the middle of your quilt, sandwiched in between the quilt top and backing fabric.

Wadding can be made from many different fibres, including bamboo, wool, cotton and polyester, as well as blends of any of these. I tend to use wadding that is a blend of recycled cotton and polyester in all my quilts. The cotton is breathable and lightweight, while the polyester gives it stability.

Loft determines how thick the wadding is; a low loft is thinner than a high loft. A low loft offers less definition to your quilting stitches and a high loft gives your quilt a more cosy look with defined stitching.

Colour

Because quilts are generally an item made for the home, looking at how the colour of your textiles can work within an interior space can be a great starting point for your projects.

Colours can also invoke an emotional response. Warm colours can be comforting or energising whereas cool colours are more serene and calming. A vibrant red, for example, may evoke strong emotions, but a warm terracotta could create a cosy, homely feeling. Lighter blues and greens can provide a restful accent to a busy room, whereas a navy or forest green may draw you into the space.

Look at the tones and values in the colours you are considering. In a neutral room, saturated colours used within an otherwise monochromatic design could create a dynamic focal point as a wallhanging or cushion and provide a sense of fun and whimsy.

A good practice to adopt when determining what colours to use is to create a palette of swatches by cutting out small sections of fabric and placing them next to each other. If you don't use that colour story in that project, store it for a later date. It may inspire you for a future quilt. There are endless possibilities, so keep trying new ways of combining colour to create quilts that you love.

Quilt care

When it comes to quiltmaking, the materials must be prepared to avoid any unfortunate mishaps later down the line. Before making a quilt, I always wash the cloth to make sure that it will not shrink once sewn. Always follow any specific care guidelines for your fabric, but as a rule of thumb, I always pre-wash new cottons and linens if they are coming off a roll. With vintage textiles the liklihood of them shrinking is lessened by their age, but always make sure they are clean before quilting with them.

Wadding can also shrink and some people recommend hand washing it before use. I don't tend to pre-wash wadding because after you have handled it and secured it with large amounts of quilting stitches it becomes quite stable. If you do choose to pre-wash your wadding, it is best to wash it by hand and then let it dry flat.

Quilts that are going to be used often will naturally soften and become worn over time. With regular use, a quilt will need to be laundered. My advice here is that you should take care when doing so, but don't worry if they shrink a small amount; that texture is what makes a quilt unique, creating that comfortable, cosy texture that you want to feel from a quilt. I tend to launder quilts on a cold wash no higher than 30°C (86°F). Avoid any bleaches or colour removers when washing coloured fabrics.

Workshops

Essential stitches and techniques

Construction

Patchwork

Appliqué

Essential stitches and techniques

WORKSHOP ONE

Here you will find all the basic stitches and hand
sewing techniques needed to get started
with quiltmaking.

KNOTTING YOUR THREAD – QUILTER'S KNOT

The quilter's knot is a neat trick for tying a quick and secure knot at the end of any sewing thread.

One — Thread the needle and wrap the end of the thread around the tip a few times – the more times you wrap, the bigger the knot – while holding the tail end of the thread to the needle.

Two — With the other hand, place your thumb and forefinger around the wrapped thread and slide it down the length of the needle towards the eye. When you reach the eye, keep sliding the wraps all the way down the length of the thread.

Three — When you reach the end of the thread, you will find the wraps naturally form a knot.

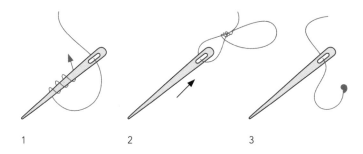

1   2   3

POPPING YOUR KNOT – HOW TO BEGIN A QUILTING STITCH

Popping the knot is a technique used in quilting to secure your thread in the quilt or project before you start your quilting stitches.

One — With the quilt top facing you, pass the needle down through the quilt top and under the wadding (batting) about 3–5 cm (1¼–2 in) away from where you want to begin stitching. Come back up through the quilt top where you want to start the stitching.

Two — Pull the needle and thread through until the knot sits on the surface of the quilt top.

Three — With your forefinger or thumb, press firmly on the fabric behind where the knot is sitting. At the same time, give the thread a short, sharp tug. The knot will pop through the weave of fabric and disappear into the wadding (batting).

Tip — This technique can be used to start your quilting stitches anywhere on your quilt top, but make sure that you secure your knot in an area that is not going to be trimmed away when the quilt is finished and bound.

Alternatively, if your row of quilting stitches starts at the edge of your quilt, you can secure your stitches by taking a couple of small overlapping stitches and tying with a knot within the seam allowance. The knot will be hidden by your binding.

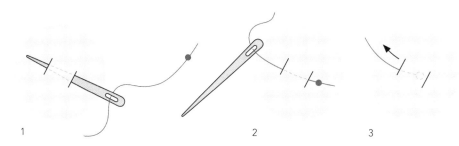

1   2   3

BASIC QUILTING STITCH

The basic stitch used in hand quilting is a running stitch (see page 34). By altering the length of your running stitches you can achieve different effects. Long stitches, spaced further apart give less definition to your quilt. Small stitches spaced close together give more defined texture. As well as experimenting with the length of your stitches, also play around with the spacing between each row of stitching.

One

Start by taking the needle one stitch length – around 0.5 cm (¼ in) – from your starting point. Insert the needle at a right angle to the quilt top and push the tip through all the layers, but do not pass the entire needle all the way through – just the tip should be visible at the back of the quilt.

Two

Now that the tip of the needle is poking through the back layer, push it along about 0.5 cm (¼ in) and rock the needle upward to bring the tip of the needle back through the layers to the top of the quilt. Bring the needle all the way through to the top and pull the thread tight to create the first stitch.

Three

Repeat this process, by taking the tip of the needle back down through the layers 0.5 cm (¼ in) away from your last stitch until you have completed a full row of stitches.

Tip

I use a length of thread that is as long as my quilt is wide, with about 20 cm (8 in) extra to tie off and secure the stitches. Find what is comfortable for you to work with.

Once you get into a rhythm and feel more comfortable with stitching, you can start to load more stitches onto the needle before pulling the thread through. This will reduce the time it takes to stitch your quilt.

When stitching in straight or curved lines, make sure to start your stitching on one side and work your way across. Alternatively, if you are stitching shapes or patterns in the quilt, make sure to begin your quilting stitches in the centre of your quilt and work outwards towards the edges. Don't be tempted to start stitching in different places as you will find that your quilt will pucker and excess fabric will form in areas of your quilt that will cause it to go out of shape and become difficult to work with.

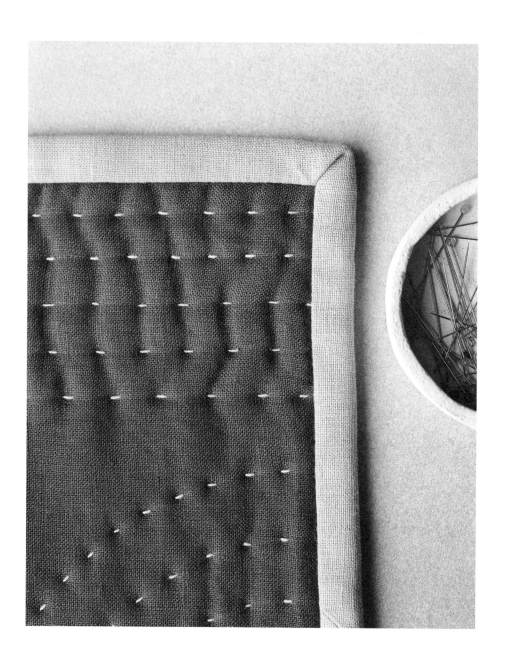

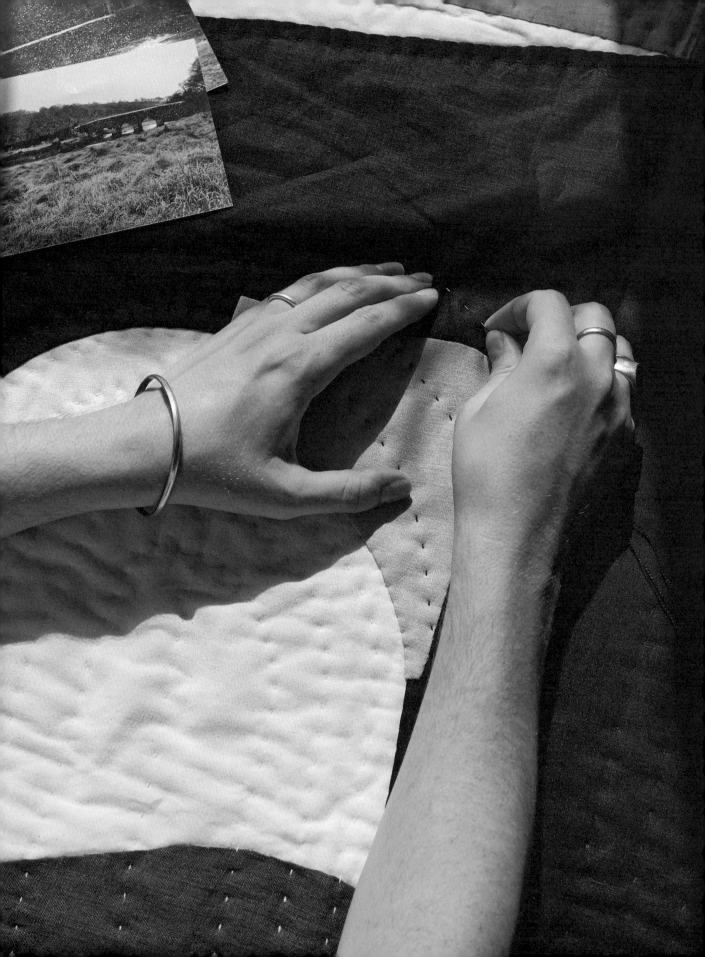

FINISHING THE STITCHING

To finish and secure your line of stitching, the thread is anchored back inside the quilt to hold it in place. The knot used to secure the thread is hidden by popping it back in between the layers.

One

When you come to your last stitch, take the needle under the top layer and wadding (batting). Come back out to the top layer and pull all of your thread through.

Two

Keeping the thread taut with one hand, wrap the needle around the thread from right to left and back through the loop formed. With the loop sitting on the surface of your quilt top, place your forefinger on top of it and pull, forming a knot that sits flush to the quilt top.

Three

Take the needle through the same hole you came out of, then slide it under the quilt top about 2.5 cm (1 in) away, bringing it back up and giving the thread a light tug. This will pop the knot back into the quilt.

Four

Snip the excess thread, being careful not to cut a hole in your fabric.

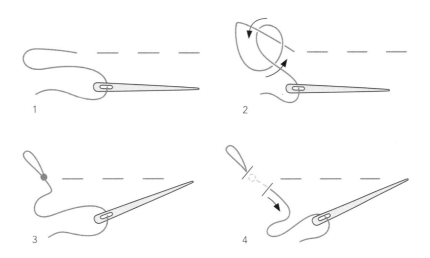

Tip

Alternatively, if your row of quilting stitches starts at the edge of your quilt, you can secure your stitches by taking a couple of small overlapping stitches and tying with a knot within the seam allowance. The knot will be hidden by your binding.

General sewing stitches

Here are four stitches you will need for stitching and finishing your quilt projects.

RUNNING STITCH

A running stitch is the most basic hand sewing stitch and can be used in multiple ways. By varying the stitch length, it can be used decoratively with large spacing or practically to sew fabric securely together with a smaller stitch spacing. Working from right to left, insert your needle into the fabric and bring it back out again. Weave your needle in and out of the fabric, keeping the stitches as even and straight as possible.

WHIP STITCH

Whip stitch is commonly used along fabric edges to join two or more layers of fabric together or to attach smaller pieces of fabric to larger pieces. Start your stitch underneath the layers of fabric and bring the needle up through all layers you wish to join, near to the edge you will be working over. Make a stitch over the edge in a diagonal direction or perpendicular to the edge, then take the needle sideways underneath and up through the fabric to make the next stitch. Repeat until the edges of the fabric are sewn together.

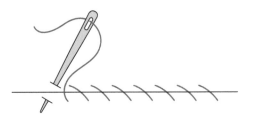

BLIND STITCH

Blind stitch is used to finish binding and attach appliqué. Your stitches should appear invisible when finished. Take a 0.5-cm (¼-in) stitch through the backing cloth, catching a few threads of the folded binding or appliqué edge. Take your needle back through the backing cloth close to where your last stitch came up. Repeat, catching a few threads of the fold each time you take a stitch. Make sure the stitches are the same length. Pull the thread taut as you go without puckering the fabric.

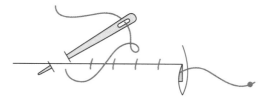

SLIP STITCH

Slip stitch is used to close openings and finish linings. It can also be used as an alternative to blind stitch. At least one neatly folded edge is necessary to work through, so that the stitches can be hidden within the fold and appear invisible when finished. With the thread secured either in the fold or backing cloth, take a small diagonal stitch through the fold and then another of the same length through the backing cloth or opposite fold. Repeat, moving along within the fold each time to create a ladder-like stitch, which, when gently tugged, will pull the two sides together.

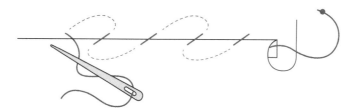

Construction

This workshop covers the foundations of
quilt construction and provides a guide to layering,
stitching and finishing a quilt with binding.

Layering and construction

A quilt is traditionally made from three layers, which are sandwiched together and secured with tacking (basting) stitches or pins to keep them in place. The 'sandwich' is then quilted together with decorative stitching, before a binding is added around the edges to complete the quilt. The layers are:

× *The quilt top* can be created from separate pieces of cloth sewn together to form a patchwork, an appliquéd cloth with decorative patches applied to the surface, strips of fabric sewn together into graphic or abstract patterns or simply a single length of exquisite fabric quilted with detailed stitch work.
× *The wadding (batting) layer* is usually slightly bigger than the quilt top to start with, and then is trimmed down after quilting.
× *The backing layer* can be made from a single length of fabric or created by piecing sections of fabric together. The backing needs to be bigger than the quilt top and wadding (batting) layers. I recommend leaving a 10–13 cm (4–5 in) margin of excess fabric along all four side of the quilt.

LAYERING YOUR QUILT

To form the foundations of the quilt you need to prepare the separate layers and 'sandwich' them together.

One
Press the quilt top and backing fabric to remove any creases. With the wrong side facing upwards, lay the backing fabric out on a clean, flat work surface. Secure the backing fabric to the work surface with strips of masking tape placed at regular intervals, keeping the fabric slightly taut with the weave as straight as possible.

Two
Place the wadding (batting) on top of the backing fabric, centering it so that there is an equal amount of excess backing fabric on all sides of the wadding. Smooth out the wadding (batting) from the middle to the outer edges, making sure that it lays flat with no creases.

Three
With the right side facing upwards, lay the quilt top over the wadding (batting), again centering it so that there is an equal amount of wadding visible on all sides of the quilt top. Smooth out the quilt top from the middle to the outer edges, making sure that it lays flat with no creases.

Stabilising the layers

Now that the quilt layers are sandwiched together in the right order, they need to be temporarily held in position to stop them sliding around or coming apart. This process is called tacking (basting) and there are two simple ways to do it.

HAND TACKING (BASTING) WITH THREAD

Tacking (basting) stitches are large running stitches made by hand, which are removed when your quilt is finished. Tacking a quilt together first, rather than pinning the layers together, allows you to work your quilting stitches and add any surface decoration without pins getting in the way.

One
Thread a slim but long needle with a large eye with an arm's length of sewing thread in a contrasting colour. Starting in the middle of the quilt top, take the needle through all three layers and secure your thread with two large stitches.

Two
Begin tacking (basting) by working a straight line of diagnonal stitches in a herringbone pattern from the centre of the quilt down to the bottom edge. Make each of the stitches about 5–8 cm (2–3 in) long. Keep the stitches tight enough that they hold the fabric taut, but not so tight that they pull the fabric. When you get to the end of a line of stitching, secure your tacking with two more large stitches worked on top of each other to hold everything in place.

Three
Work another line of diagonal stitches from the centre to the top edge. Then work another line from the centre to the right edge, and then again from the centre to the left edge.

Four
Depending on the size of your quilt, continue to work horizontal rows of diagonal stitches from the centre out to the right or left edges to build up a grid of tacking (basting). Repeat with any vertical rows as necessary.

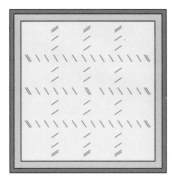

You can also tack (baste) a quilt using quilter's safety pins, which are slightly curved to help them go through the layers of your quilt. Start in the centre of the quilt and smooth the layers as you pin towards all the edges. Place a pin every 10–20 cm (4–8 in) apart, depending on how big your quilt is. The more pins you use, the more stable and secure the quilt layers will be.

Quilting

Quilting refers to the stitching that is used to hold the separate quilt layers together. Stitching a quilt can be done either by machine or hand; in this book the focus is on hand quilting. Traditionally, the basic hand quilting stitch is a running stitch (see page 34) that can be used to create multiple, parallel lines or intricate patterns that travel across the quilt.

Marking the quilt for stitching

When quilting in lines, straight lines, curved lines or other shapes across the quilt, you may need to mark temporary guidelines for the stitching using a quilter's crease, low-tack tape, tailor's chalk or other type of erasable marker or fabric pen (see pages 16–19 for more information). The patterns made by the quilting stitches can either complement or contrast the lines and shapes of the quilt top, but bear in mind that close lines of stitching will create a greater variation in depth, depending on the thickness of the wadding (batting).

To mark a straight line of stitching, work off an existing vertical or horizontal edge and, using a ruler or straight edge, score the line with a crease tool or mark the line with low-tack masking tape. When marking the first line of quilting stitches, make sure you account for the binding and include the width of the binding in your first measurement. If you want to create an even number of lines, measure your quilt length and divide that measurement by the number of rows of stitching you want to achieve.

For curved lines and other shapes, draw guidelines freehand or trace around a template with tailor's chalk or an erasable marker or fabric pen.

Binding

Binding is the process of concealing the raw edges of your quilt to tidy it up and keep it from coming apart. Adding a binding is a multi-step exercise and on most of my quilts I use a straight, twofold binding to frame the quilt with a neat border.

Twofold binding

Twofold binding is a folded strip of fabric that is attached to the right side of the quilt top and then turned under and hand-stitched to the backing fabric. It is one of the most common ways of binding a quilt and creates a beautiful, long-lasting finish to the work. To calculate how much binding you will need, measure the four sides of your quilt, add the measurements together and then add on another 60 cm (23½ in).

MAKING YOUR OWN BINDING

One
Fold the length of fabric in half widthways, selvedge to selvedge, and press along the fold.

Two
Lay the folded fabric on a cutting mat. Using a quilter's rule, mark out a series of strips each 7.5 cm (3 in) wide across the width of the fabric. Cut along the marked lines to create long, straight strips once unfolded.

Three
To join the strips together, take the short edge of two strips and, with right sides together, layer one strip over the other to create a right angle. Pin the two pieces in place making sure to overlap them by about 1 cm (⅜ in) on each side.

Four
Sew the two strips together with a diagonal line, and trim off the excess fabric – those little triangles on each side – so you have a straight edge. Press the seam open. Repeat this process until all of your strips are sewn together, forming one long strip.

Five
Fold this long strip in half lengthways. Press along the folded edge to create a continous length of binding ready to attach to your quilt.

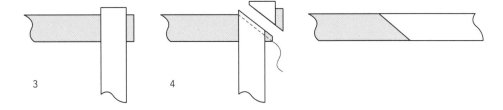

3

4

Make sure when sewing the strips together that all your seams are on the same side of your binding.

Bindings don't have to be one colour; you can add strips made from different colours or prints to create some interesting bindings.

ATTACHING BINDING

One

Trim the edges of the quilt by cutting any excess wadding (batting) and backing fabric away from the sides, using the edge of the quilt top as a guide.

Two

With the right side of the quilt top facing upwards and the right side of the binding facing downwards, align one raw edge of the binding with the raw edge of the quilt starting from one corner and working all along one side.

Three

With a sewing machine, begin stitching two-thirds of the way down from the corner where the binding starts. This will leave a tail of binding that will be used to join the two ends of the binding later on. Sew the binding to the quilt with a 1-cm (⅜-in) seam allowance.

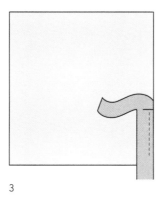

3

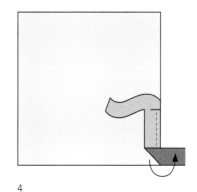

4

Four	When you get to the first corner, stop stitching 1 cm (⅜ in) away from the edge and back stitch to secure your stitching. Lift the needle and take your quilt off of the sewing machine. Fold the binding up and away from the quilt at a right angle, keeping the edge of the binding in line with the edge of the quilt.
Five	Holding the fold in place, create a mitred corner by bringing the binding back down, over the corner fold so that the raw edge of the binding lines up with the next side of your quilt. Machine stitch the binding all along this next edge of the quilt, as before.
Six	Repeat steps 4–5 for all the remaining corners until you return to the side of the quilt that you started on.
Seven	Carry on stitching the binding to this side of your quilt, stopping about one-third of the way from where you started stitching the binding after leaving a tail. Back stitch to keep your binding in place and take your quilt off the sewing machine.

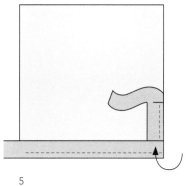

5

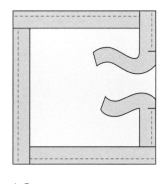

6–7

JOINING THE BINDING

One — The binding is now attached all the way around the quilt, apart from the gap between where you started and stopped stitching. You will have two long tails of excess binding, one on each side of the gap. Find the centre of the gap and mark it with a pin or chalk.

Two — Starting on the left side of the opening, take the tail of binding and lay it flat to the top of the quilt, over the marked centre point. Mark the binding in the same place as the mark on the quilt.

Three — From the mark on the binding, measure a distance that is the same measurement as the width of the folded binding and draw a line. For example: if the folded binding is 3.75 cm (1½ in) wide, measure 3.75 cm (1½ in) from your mark. Make sure to draw the line to the right of your mark.

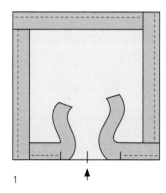

1

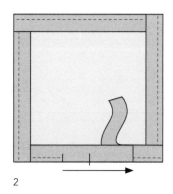

2

Four — Trim the binding along the line you have now marked.

Five — Repeat steps 1–4 on the right-hand side of the opening.

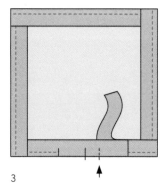

3

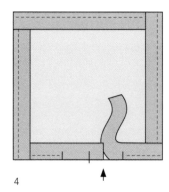

4

Six	Now that you have trimmed both ends of the binding, open out the tail on the right-hand side with the right side of the fabric facing up. Open out the left-hand side of the binding so that the wrong side of the fabric is facing you. Overlap the two ends of the binding to make a right angle with the edges aligned and with right sides together.
Seven	Pin the ends together and then sew a line of stitching across the corner. Now is a good time to check that you have sewn it together correctly. Fold the binding back in half and check that it lies flat against the edge of the quilt.
Eight	Once you are happy that it is sewn correctly, trim away the excess binding fabric at the corner, leaving a 1-cm (⅜-in) seam allowance.
Nine	Press the corner seam open, and then fold the binding back in half. You should have one continuous strip of binding that fits perfect flush to the edge of the quilt.
Ten	Lay the seam binding flat along the unstitched gap, aligning the raw edge with the quilt, and finish stitching it down with a 1-cm (⅜-in) seam allowance. The binding is now fully attached all the way around the edges of the quilt.

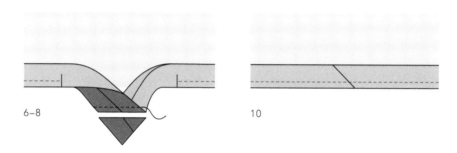

6–8

10

HAND FINISHING THE BINDING

To finish the quilt the binding is folded over the edge and hand sewn to the backing fabric with a blind stitch (see page 35). This covers all raw edges and completes the quilt with a beautiful invisible finish.

One

Thread a needle with a length of strong sewing thread that matches the colour of your binding and knot one end. Start your stitching around 20 cm (8 in) from one corner of the quilt. Secure the thread within the underside of the binding by bringing the needle through the fold in the binding and stitching a few small stitches to hold in place.

Two

Fold the binding over to the back of the quilt, enclosing the raw edges of the quilt top, wadding (batting) and backing fabric. The edge of your binding should overlap the line of machine stitching, which you can use as a guide to sew the binding down.

Three

To begin stitching the binding down and with the back of the quilt facing you, start by taking the needle in through the backing fabric of your quilt and work blind stitch (see page 35) until you reach the corner. Make sure you are not sewing through all three layers – the stitching should not show on the front of the quilt.

Four

At the corner, fold the edge of your binding over to form a mitre. Use your fingers to even out the fold so that it creates a neat 45-degree angle, then complete the blind stitch around the corner to hold it in place. You can add a few extra stitches in the very corner to strengthen it.

Five

Continue until you have stitched down the binding all the way around the edges of your quilt and secure your thread with a few back stitches and a knot.

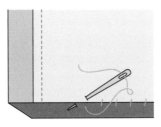

3

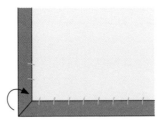

4–5

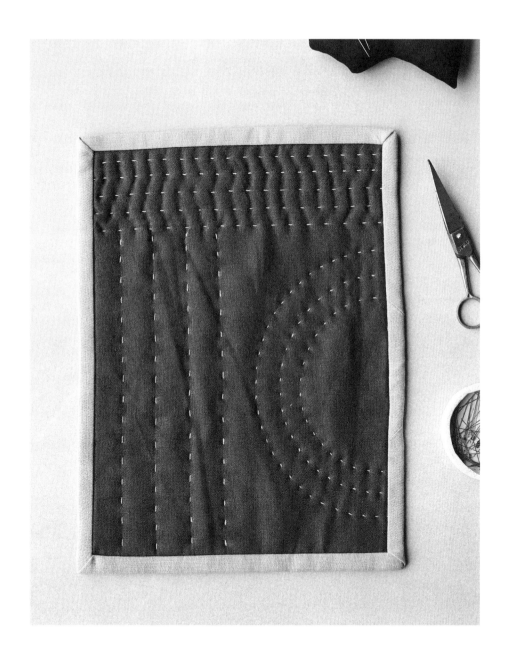

Self-binding

Self-binding is a good technique for smaller quilts and projects. Rather than trimming the backing fabric to the size of the quilt top and wadding (batting), to self-bind you need to make sure that there is at least 5 cm (2 in) of excess backing fabric around all four sides of your quilt.

One — Start by trimming the wadding (batting) layer in line with the edge of the quilt top, but do not trim the backing fabric. To do this, fold the backing fabric underneath and away from the edge of the quilt. Once you have trimmed the wadding (batting), fold the backing fabric back into position.

Two — Press the edges of the backing fabric over onto itself so that the wrong sides are together and the raw edge of the backing fabric lines up with the raw edge of the quilt, creating a single fold all the way around. Fold the pressed edge of the backing fabric border in over the quilt edge so that it lays flat on the quilt top and pin in place.

Three — With a fine sewing needle and strong sewing thread, slip stitch (see page 35) the binding down to the top of your quilt, being careful not to catch the back of your quilt as you go. When you get to a corner, neatly fold the binding, overlapping the folded edges and hand stitching them in place.

Patchwork

Patchwork is a process in which small pieces of cloth in different patterns, colours or textures are sewn together. This workshop shows you how to use different patchwork techniques to create modern quilts: piecing designs, creating blocks and joining them all together.

Patchwork basics

The patchwork techniques I cover in this book are inspired by improvisational quilting techniques (commonly known as 'improv' quilting), as well as traditional quiltmaking processes. Because I like to experiment with both, I use the term 'informal' quilting as a way to acknowledge these areas of quiltmaking in my work. Sometimes a patchwork might line up in crisp lines or repeat patterns, and other times it might be formed by undulating curves that travel across the surface of the quilt. The techniques in this workshop are the ones that I most commonly use, and I hope that by sharing them with you, you can expand on them and use them in new and interesting ways.

Free-form patchwork

Free-form patchwork is created by sewing pieces of fabric together without pre-cutting them all to the same shape and size. You will need a selection of fabric scraps in different sizes.

One — Trim the scraps to clean up the edges so they are ready to be joined together. Place two similar-size scraps of fabric right sides together and aligned along one edge. Machine stitch together with a 1-cm (⅜-in) seam allowance. Press the seam open.

Two — Lay the joined fabric pieces flat on a cutting mat. Using a rotary cutter and ruler, trim the edge so that it is straight and level. You can trim the edge at an angle, but it needs to be straight.

Three — Find another scrap that is the same size or longer than the two joined pieces. Place it on top of the joined pieces, with right sides together and one edge aligned with the trimmed edge of the original piece. Sew the pieces together with a 1-cm (⅜-in) seam allowance and press the seam open, as before.

Four — Trim the edges of the new piece so that they are in line with the edges of the original piece. Keep adding new scraps of fabric, pressing open the seams and trimming as you go, until you are happy with the size and composition of the patchwork.

Five — Once you have added four or five pieces and grown your patchwork to a manageable size, it becomes a 'block'. Continue to make more blocks and then sew them together into a quilt top. Add interest to your patchwork by sewing sections to your 'block' that are made up of several other pieces of fabric. Each new piece is joined to the last edge that you trimmed.

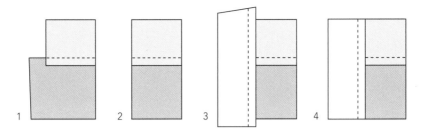

Strip patchwork

Strip patchwork blocks are created by joining strips of fabric together to create a new length of fabric. These lengths can then be joined together in different ways, alternating the strips or integrating them into your larger quilt designs.

One — Take two lengths of fabric of similar size but different colours. Place one on top of the other with right sides facing upwards.

Two — With a rotary cutter, cut strips across the width of the layered fabric. By doing this free hand without using a ruler you will create slightly irregular strips. If you prefer your strips to be more regular, use a quilting rule to cut straight lines. When cutting out the strips, allow for a 1-cm (⅜-in) seam allowance on all sides you are planning to join together.

Three — After cutting the fabrics, separate the layers and and lay out the strips adjacent in a row, alternating the colours. Play around with the angles to make sure that the block will be fairly square after sewing the strips together.

Four — Place the first two strips right sides together and sew with a 1-cm (⅜-in) seam allowance to join. Press the seam open. Repeat to add the other strips. Once all the strips are stitched together, lay the block on a cutting mat. Using a rotary cutter and quilter's rule, trim the block to size. Multiple blocks can then be sewn together to become a quilt top.

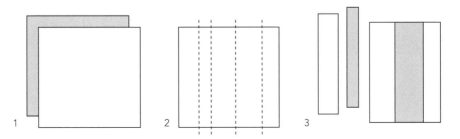

Curved patchwork

Sewing curves can be daunting even to seasoned patchworkers, and if you are new to sewing, a curved seam may sound tricky. By following a few simple steps, you will soon be able to master the art of joining curves with ease. Here are three different techniques for you to try.

CURVED PATCHWORK BLOCKS – CUTTING METHOD

To create natural-looking, organic curves you will need two pieces of fabric that are similar in size and shape but in different colours. The cutting method results in a final block that is smaller than the original fabric, so make sure the fabric pieces are at least 5 cm (2 in) larger than the size you want the final block to be once trimmed.

One	Take two lengths of fabric of similar size but different colours. Place one on top of the other with right sides facing upwards.
Two	Using a rotary cutter, cut a curve freehand from one corner of the fabric to another, cutting through both layers. The curve can be cut in any direction across the fabric.
Three	Separate all the fabric pieces. Now match the inner curve of one colour with the outer curve of the other colour to create two blocks, each made up of contrasting colours.
Four	Using tailor's chalk or an erasable marker or fabric pen, draw a series of marks across the curves so that they match up on both pieces of fabric.

 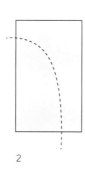   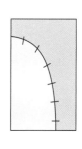

1   2   3   4

Five	With right sides facing, pin the two pieces of fabric together along the curve, matching up the marks.
Six	Folding the concave/outer curve on top of the convex/inner curve, stitch the pieces together with a 0.5-cm (¼-in) seam allowance, slowly feeding the fabric through the sewing machine and matching up the raw edges.
Seven	Press the curve on the wrong side. When pressing a curve with a 0.5-cm (¼-in) seam allowance, press in the direction that it naturally wants to fall. Turn your sewn piece over and press again on the right side, making sure your curved seam is flat. Trim the uneven sides of your block to complete your curved patchwork.
Eight	Using a rotary cutter and quilter's rule, trim any uneven sides to neaten your completed curved patchwork block.

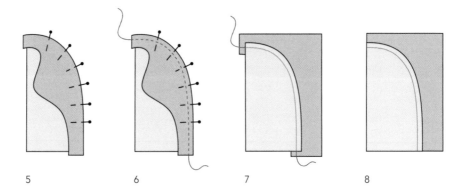

5 6 7 8

CURVED PATCHWORK BLOCKS – STRIP METHOD

Curved patchwork strip blocks are made in a similar way to the strip patchwork block technique described on page 55. Here, each strip is cut and joined with a gentle curve to create a wave-like effect.

One — Lay two strips of fabric on a cutting mat with right sides facing upwards. Overlap the strips along the edge that you want to join together. The overlap has to be the width of the curve that you want to create.

Two — Using a rotary cutter, cut a long, shallow curved line through both layers of fabric.

Three — Place the two pieces of fabric with right sides together and curved edges aligned. Sew together with a 1-cm (⅜-in) seam allowance, following the line of the curve.

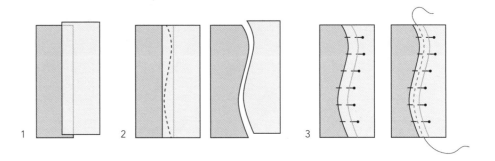

Four — Press the joined pieces on the wrong side, pressing the seam to the left or right and following the line of the curve. Turn the pieces over and press again on the right side using steam.

Five — Repeat steps 1–4 with another piece of fabric, layering it over the edge of the first and cutting a curved line. Sew the pieces together and press the seams flat, as before.

Six — Keep adding more pieces with curved seams to create the size block you want. When all the pieces are joined together, trim the edges of the block to the required size.

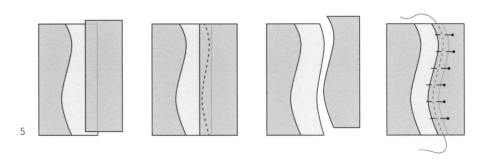

CURVED PATCHWORK BLOCKS – APPLIQUÉ METHOD

Another way to create curved patchwork blocks is by using this appliqué method – pre-pressed curved shapes are applied to the surface of the fabric and attached with an appliqué stitch. Once secured the work is turned over and the excess fabric is trimmed away, transforming something that started off as an appliqué into patchwork. This process is really good for working small curves and intricate designs.

One	Cut out 15-cm (6-in) squares from two different colour fabrics. Draw a curve from edge to edge across one of the coloured squares.
Two	Cut along your drawn line, so that you are cutting the square in half along the curve.
Three	Pick one half of the cut square and press a 1-cm (⅜-in) fold along the edge of the curve, turning the fabric to the wrong side.
Four	Lay this pressed half on top of the complete square, both with right sides facing upwards and with the outer edges aligned. You should now have what looks like one square with a curved line going through it.
Five	Pin the two layers together. Using a blind stitch (see page 35), stitch along the folded line of the curve to attach the two layers together.
Six	Once you have finished stitching, turn the square over to the wrong side and cut away the excess fabric from the lower square underneath the top layer. Use the turned-over seam allowance as a guide. Now you have a perfectly neat, curved patchwork block.

  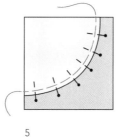 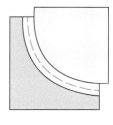

1   5   6

Joining patchwork blocks

Once you have a selection of patchwork blocks ready to be joined, it is time to put them together to form a quilt top. To achieve a straight, neat edge when joining blocks together, use a rotary cutter with a quilter's rule or straight edge to trim up the edges of the blocks before joining them.

One

Place a quilter's rule or straight edge on one side of the first block where you want to trim to a straight line. Using a rotary cutter, trim the edge of the block along the rule to neaten.

Two

Now that you have the first straight edge, use this a guide to neaten the other three edges into a square or rectangle. Line up the trimmed edge with one of the registration lines on the quilter's rule. Once the quilter's rule is square, neaten the second side with the rotary cutter. Repeat this process all the way around your block.

Three

Once you have squared up all of your blocks to their desired sizes, join the first two together with a 1-cm (⅜-in) seam allowance. Press open the seam. Repeat the process until all of the blocks are joined together.

Tip

You can also use curved seams to join two finished blocks together, creating organic lines and joins across the quilt top. To do this, follow the same instructions to create a curved strip block (see page 60) but instead of layering plain fabrics to create your curves, layer the block edges on top of each other to create a curved joining seam.

Trimming patchwork quilt tops

Once your patchwork quilt top is complete, it might need to be trimmed down in preparation for the next stage of the quiltmaking process.

Select the side of the quilt top that you feel is the neatest. Using a quilter's rule or straight edge, mark a straight line along this edge of the quilt top. Using this drawn line as a guide, mark another line along the second edge of the quilt top at a right angle to the first line. Repeat this step to draw another line on the third edge. Mark a final, fourth line on the remaining edge of the quilt top. Using a rotary cutter and quilter's rule or straight edge, trim the quilt top following the marked guidelines.

Tip

After you have trimmed your quilt top, you may find you have cut through some of the stitching that joins the blocks together. I run a few additional stitches over the joins on the sewing machine to hold them in place. I do this within the seam allowance so that it will not be visible on the final quilt.

Appliqué

WORKSHOP FOUR

Appliqué is the process of layering fabric shapes over a larger piece of cloth and attaching them to the surface. It is a way of bringing life to a quilt, adding extra dimensions to a piece. Instead of seaming the fabric pieces into the quilt top as you do with patchwork, appliqué allows you to collage layers of additional shapes, textures and colours onto the surface of your quilt design, in any pattern you choose.

Appliqué techniques

For the projects in this book, and for those that I make at House of Quinn, appliqué is worked using a turned edge – a technique whereby you turn the raw edge of the appliqué fabric under to create a neat edge before stitching it to the base cloth. This workshop covers how to use templates and freehand processes to create shapes and patterns that you can apply to your quilt tops.

Turned-edge appliqué – using a template

Using a template made from freezer paper is a simple way to achieve a neat finish and makes turning under the raw edges of the appliqué shapes much easier. Freezer paper can be used multiple times, so store the templates ready to be reused.

One	Draw your chosen shapes on the matt side of the freezer paper – these can be drawn freehand or traced around household objects – and then cut them out using paper scissors. They are now the templates for your appliqué.
Two	Make a selection of fabric scraps to use for your appliqué. They need to be at least 1 cm (⅜ in) bigger than the templates all the way around.
Three	Place one template, with the shiny (waxed) side down, onto the wrong side of one of the fabric scraps. Using the iron, with the steam setting turned off, press the template to fuse it to the fabric.
Four	Once the template has fused to the fabric, trim the edges of the fabric scrap leaving at least a 1-cm (⅜-in) border all the way around the edge of the template.
Five	Carefully press the fabric border over the edge of the template to the wrong side. If your shape has corners, fold these over and in on themselves to create neat edges.
Six	Once you have pressed all the edges under, carefully remove the paper template and turn the shape over. With the edges all turned under, press the shape using steam to help them stay in place. The turned-edge appliqué shape is now ready for sewing.

To create larger shapes, draw them onto the fabric freehand. Using chalk or a chalk pen, draw the shape on the wrong side of the fabric. Cut the shape out, with a 1-cm (⅜-in) seam allowance all the way around the drawn outline. Press the seam allowance under as instructed in steps 5 and 6.

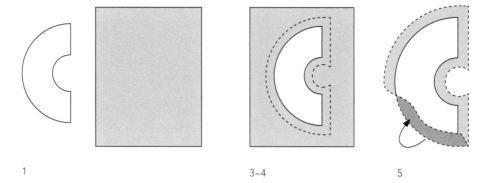

1   3–4   5

Attaching appliqué – with invisible stitching

Appliqué can be attached to the surface of a quilt with many different stitch techniques; to create a neat edge around the fabric shapes I prefer to use an invisible stitch, known as blind stitch (see page 35). Before the appliqué shapes can be stitched onto the base cloth, they must first be secured in position. Do this with large tacking (basting) stitches (see page 40) around 3–5 cm (1¼–2 in) long worked all the way around the edge of the appliqué piece.

One | Thread a fine needle with a length of sewing thread that matches the colour of the appliqué piece. Tie a knot in the end of the thread.

Two | Before you start stitching, you need to hide the knot in the fold of the turned-edge appliqué piece. To do this, bring the needle out through the creased fold of the appliqué shape from the inside, so the knot is held securely in the fold.

Three | Using blind stitches no longer than 0.5 cm (¼ in), stitch the edges of appliqué shape to the base cloth. Tug the thread taut as you complete each stitch to secure.

Four | Stitch all the way around the appliqué shape until you reach the starting point. Secure the stitches by making 2 or 3 tiny stitches on top of one another on the edge of the appliqué shape. Push the needle under the edge of the appliqué shape in the same place as the finishing stitches, take the needle to the centre of the shape and bring the needle back out to the front. Trim the thread so that it disappears between the appliqué shape and the base cloth.

Tip | When adding appliqué to a quilt, you can stitch your fabric shapes to the quilt top before or after you have sandwiched your quilts layers together – just make sure to stitch your appliqué to the quilt top and not through all three layers of the quilt.

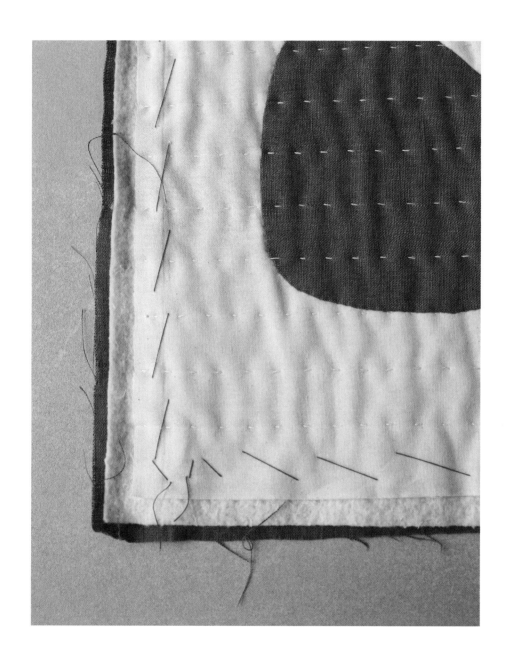

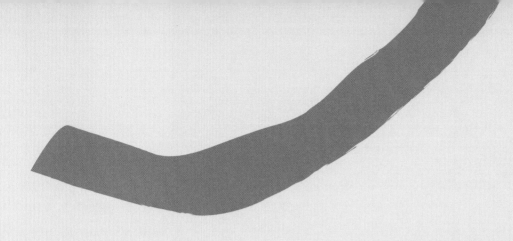

Projects

COLOUR BLOCK QUILT

The Colour Block Quilt is inspired by the informal patchwork techniques that I love to use in the studio. By combining this relaxed approach with a selective colour palette you can create bold and dynamic quilt compositions that look beautiful in any room in the house. This is a great project for using up larger lengths of spare fabric or odd remnants that you may have hoarded away.

Size: 120 x 140 cm (47¼ x 55 in). You can adjust the finished size, but you will need to calculate the amount of fabric needed.

MATERIALS

Quilt top fabric: Approx. 60 cm (23½ in) of 150-cm (59-in) wide cotton or linen in each of three main colours. Approx. 20 x 70 cm (8 x 27½ in) of cotton or linen for accent colour. Excess fabric can be used to make the binding.

Backing fabric: 150 cm (1¾ yd) of 150-cm (59-in) wide cotton or linen, or piece together smaller sections of fabric to create a backing at least 10 cm (4 in) wider and longer than the quilt top.

Wadding (batting): 130 x 150 cm (51¼ x 59 in), or at least 5 cm (2 in) wider and longer than the finished quilt.

Binding: At least 6 m (6¾ yd) of 7.5-cm (3 in) wide straight binding in colour of your choice (see pages 42–49).

Sewing thread: Strong sewing thread in matching or contrasting colour to the fabric.

Quilting thread: 10 g ball of pearl cotton crochet thread size 8 or similar in a colour of your choice.

TOOLS AND EQUIPMENT

Quilter's rule
Tailor's chalk, fabric marker or quilter's crease
Fabric scissors
Rotary cutter and cutting mat
Sewing machine
Sewing needles and quilting needles
Iron and ironing board

QUILT PLAN

This Colour Block Quilt is divided into four strip blocks across the width of the quilt. Each strip block is made up of smaller fabric panels, which are joined together in turn. Once the four strips are completed, they are lined up and sewn together to form the final quilt top. Use the quilt plan below as a guide when deciding which of your colours to use for each panel in the strip blocks.

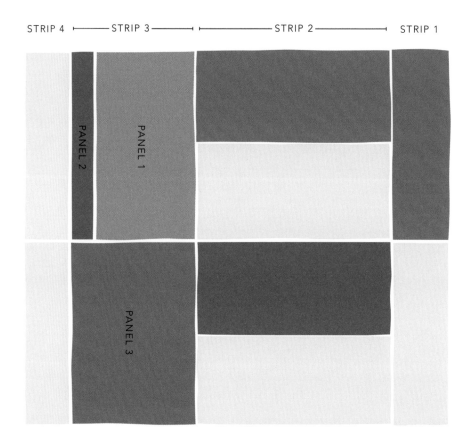

STRIP 4 ⊢——— STRIP 3 ———⊣ ⊢——————— STRIP 2 ———————⊣ STRIP 1

PANEL 2

PANEL 1

PANEL 3

MAKING THE STRIP BLOCKS

One

For strip one, cut two panels of fabric measuring 62 x 22 cm (24⅜ x 3¾ in) including seam allowances. With right sides together, join the two panels along one short side with a 1-cm (⅜-in) seam allowance. Press the seam open. Repeat for strip four.

Two	For strip two, cut four panels of fabric measuring 32 x 62 cm (12½ x 24⅜ in) including seam allowances. With right sides together, join the first panel to the second panel along one long side with 1-cm (⅜-in) seam allowance. Press the seam open. Repeat for the third and fourth panels. Join the two sets of panels, as before, and press the seam open.
Three	For strip three, cut three panels in the following sizes including seam allowance:

× Panel one: 62 x 32 cm (24⅜ x 12½ in)
× Panel two: 62 x 12 cm (24⅜ x 4¾ in)
× Panel three: 62 x 42 cm (24⅜ x 16½ in)

Four	With right sides together, join panel one to panel two along one long side with a 1-cm (⅜-in) seam allowance. With right sides together, join the stitched panels to panel three along the short (42-cm/16½-in) side with a 1-cm (⅜-in) seam allowance. Press the seam open.

ASSEMBLING THE QUILT TOP

One	Following the quilt plan opposite, join the four strips in order with a 1-cm (⅜-in) seam allowance, taking care to line up the centre seams down all the strips.

CONSTRUCTING AND FINSHING THE QUILT

One	Construct the quilt by assembling the layers (see pages 38–41) and stitching with quilting stitches (see pages 30 and 34–35) as desired.
Two	Bind the edges of the quilt with the pre-prepared binding strip (see pages 42–49).

Tip	When lining up your strips to form the quilt top design, it doesn't really matter if the seam lines don't match up. It makes for a more informal look.
	If you want to vary the design, sew your finished strips in a different order or change the size of the panels. It is completely up to you.

LEY LINES QUILT

The Ley Lines Quilt is inspired by the first collection of quilts I ever made, using leftover cotton and fabric repurposed from garment toiles. This is a great quilt for experimenting with scale and playing with the idea of negative space; each time you use this technique to create a quilt you can come up with another combination. I love to restrict the colour palette to two key colours and one accent fabric. In this version of the quilt, I have used a monochromatic palette with midnight blue accents.

Size: 140 x 190 cm (55 x 75 in). You can adjust the finished size, but you will need to calculate the amount of fabric needed.

MATERIALS

Quilt top fabric: Approx. 100 cm (1⅛ yd) of 150-cm (59-in) wide cotton or linen in each of two main colours. Approx. 50 cm (20 in) of 150-cm (59-in) wide fabric in an accent colour.

Backing fabric: 200 cm (2¼ yd) of 150-cm (59-in) wide cotton or linen, or piece together smaller sections of fabric to create a backing 10 cm (4 in) wider and longer than the quilt top.

Wadding (batting): 200 x 150 cm (2¼ yd x 59 in), or at least 5 cm (2 in) wider and longer than the finished quilt.

Binding: At least 7.5 m (8¼ yd) of 7.5-cm (3-in) wide straight binding in colour of your choice (see pages 42–49).

Sewing thread: Strong sewing thread in matching or contrasting colour to the fabric.

Quilting thread: 10 g ball of pearl cotton crochet thread size 8 or similar in each of two colours of your choice.

TOOLS AND EQUIPMENT

Quilter's rule
Tailor's chalk, fabric marker or quilter's crease
Fabric scissors
Rotary cutter and cutting mat
Sewing machine
Sewing needles and quilting needles
Iron and ironing board

QUILT PLAN

The Ley Lines Quilt is constructed in strip blocks that run across the width of the quilt. These strip blocks are created by joining smaller pieces of fabric in a row, placing the two main colours in each of the strip blocks so that when joined they create the ley lines or meandering road that travels down the quilt top. Decide which of the main colours will be the travelling colour and which will be the negative space. Sometimes the ley line or road will come to a dead end, which is then highlighted by your third accent colour.

MAKING THE STRIP BLOCKS

One

Following your quilt plan, cut fabric panels from all three colours in varying widths to make up the strip blocks for your quilt. Each strip block can vary in height, but all the panels within the same strip block must be the same height. When the panels are joined with a 1-cm (⅜-in) seam allowance, each strip block needs to measure 142 cm (56 in) wide (or your chosen quilt width plus 2 cm/¾ in), so allow for the seam allowances when cutting out the panels. When all the strip blocks are joined with a 1-cm (⅜-in) seam allowance, the quilt top needs to measure 192 cm (75¾ in) long (or your chosen quilt length plus 2 cm/¾ in).

Two	Lay out all the fabric panels in their strip blocks according to your quilt plan to make sure you are happy with the arrangement. Make sure that panels of the ley line colour (which is black for the quilt pictured here) partially line up when the strip blocks are laid in rows – this is to connect each strip block visually with the colour travelling through the rows down the quilt. Intersperse small panels of the accent colour (I chose blue for the quilt pictured here) every now and then, but not necessarily in every row.
Three	For strip one, with right sides together, join the first two panels along one short side with a 1-cm (⅜-in) seam allowance. Join all the subsequent panels in the same way to complete the strip block. Press all the seams open.
Four	For all the remaining strips, join the panels in the same way to create strip blocks of varying heights.

ASSEMBLING THE QUILT TOP

One	Following your quilt plan, join the strip blocks in order with a 1-cm (⅜-in) seam allowance.

CONSTRUCTING AND FINISHING THE QUILT

One	Construct the quilt by assembling the layers (see pages 38–41) and stitching with quilting stitches (see pages 30 and 34–35) as desired.
Two	Bind the edges of the quilt with the pre-prepared binding strip (see pages 42–49).

Tip	When arranging the colours in each strip, I like to work to the rule of two-thirds main colours and one-third accent colour, but on some strips you can skip the accent colour altogether.
	I have stitched my quilt with stitch lines that travel in different directions to add another layer of detail to the final design.

ABSTRACT QUILT

This quilt was inspired by walks under the white chalk cliffs of the south east coast of England, from Brighton to Saltdean. By using neutral tones in a quilt you can create a bold abstract design that won't overwhelm its surroundings. This is a great way to add textile warmth to a room without introducing too much strong colour.

Size: 120 x 120 cm (47¼ x 47¼ in). You can adjust the finished size, but you will need to calculate the amount of fabric needed.

MATERIALS

Quilt top fabric: Approx. 50 cm (20 in) of 150-cm (59-in) or 114-cm (45-in) wide cotton or linen in each of four neutral colours. This quilt can be made from lots of fabric scraps to reuse textiles.

Backing fabric: 130 x 130 cm (51¼ x 51¼ in) of cotton or linen, or piece together smaller sections of fabric to create a backing at least 10 cm (4 in) wider and longer than the quilt top.

Wadding (batting): 130 x 130 cm (51¼ x 51¼ in), or at least 5 cm (2 in) wider and longer than the finished quilt.

Binding: At least 5.5 m (6 yd) of 7.5-cm (3-in) wide, straight binding in colour of your choice (see pages 42–49).

Sewing thread: Strong sewing thread in matching or contrasting colour to the fabric.

Quilting thread: 10 g ball of pearl cotton crochet thread size 8 or similar in colour of your choice.

TOOLS AND EQUIPMENT

Quilter's rule
Tailor's chalk, fabric marker or quilter's crease
Fabric scissors
Rotary cutter and cutting mat
Sewing machine
Sewing needles and quilting needles
Iron and ironing board

QUILT PLAN

The Abstract Quilt is created by collaging smaller pieces of fabric together, creating a seemingly random pattern. The design looks complex at first glance, but this quilt is broken down into five different-sized blocks that are then joined together to create the informal arrangement of colours. Each block is made slightly larger than the size required and then trimmed, before sewing the blocks together to form the quilt top.

BLOCK 5

BLOCK 1

BLOCK 3

BLOCK 4

BLOCK 2

MAKING THE PATCHWORK BLOCKS

One
Cut the four quilt top fabrics into rectangles of various random sizes.

Two
Take two fabric rectangles roughly the same size in any colours. With right sides together, join them along one side with a 1-cm (⅜ in) seam allowance. Press the seam open.

Three
Take another fabric rectangle that is roughly equal in size to the newly joined piece and join these with right sides together and a 1-cm (⅜ in) seam. Press the seam open.

Four	Using a quilter's rule and rotary cutter, trim the sides of the patch so that the third piece sits flush with the first two pieces of fabric, creating a new straight edge to grow your patchwork onto.
Five	Repeat steps 3–4 in order to grow your patchwork, joining and trimming each new fabric piece as before, but alternating the colours as you sew.
Six	Some fabric pieces can be joined on an angle, rather than along a straight line. Using a quilter's rule and rotary cutter, cut an angle into one side of a fabric piece. Take another piece that is at least twice as wide as the angled piece. With right sides together, join the two pieces along the angled edge with a 1-cm (⅜-in) seam allowance. Press the seam open. Trim away the excess fabric, levelling up the sides of the pieces to straighten.
Seven	Use the same technique as outlined in step 6 to add new fabric pieces at an angle to patches already sewn together. Using a quilter's rule and rotary cutter, cut across the seam of the joined pieces at an angle. With right sides together, join the new fabric piece to the cut angled edge with a 1-cm (⅜-in) seam allowance.
Eight	Continue joining fabric pieces either at an angle or on a straight line to create a patchwork block. Play around with the composition and alternate the colours as you grow your block. Make enough blocks to make up the size of quilt desired.

ASSEMBLING THE QUILT TOP

One	Once you have enough blocks to cover an area slightly larger than the size of the quilt top, trim each block to straighten all the sides.
Two	With right sides together, join the blocks with a 1-cm (⅜-in) seam allowance to make up the quilt top in the desired size.

CONSTRUCTING AND FINISHING THE QUILT

One	Construct the quilt by assembling the layers (see pages 38–41) and stitching with quilting stitches (see pages 30 and 34–35) as desired.
Two	Bind the edges of the quilt with the pre-prepared binding strip (see pages 42–49).

Tip	I tend to work on smaller blocks of five or six pieces of fabric at a time, then join these together to create five big blocks that are then joined to make the quilt top.

FORAGER BAG

The Forager Bag was inspired by the foraging trips of my childhood. It is a handy bag for collecting all those interesting things you might find while wandering the countryside. The short, bucket-style bag with a crossbody strap is easy to create from small scraps and makes a really great project to use up any remnants or fabrics you have left over from bigger projects.

Size: 57 x 18 cm (22 x 7 in) excluding strap.

MATERIALS

Outer bag fabric: Enough scraps or remnants of cotton or linen in two or more contrasting colours to make a 59 x 20-cm (23¼ x 8-in) patchwork block.

Bag base, strap and lining fabric: 50 cm (20 in) of 150-cm (59-in) wide cotton or linen.

Wadding (batting): 64 x 25 cm (25¼ x 9½ in), or at least 5 cm (2 in) wider and longer than outer bag template.

Sewing thread: Strong sewing thread in matching or contrasting colour to the fabric.

Quilting thread: 10 g ball of pearl cotton crochet thread size 8 or similar in a colour of your choice.

Paper for templates: 60 x 40-cm (24 x 16-in) piece of dot-and-cross pattern paper or brown parcel paper.

TOOLS AND EQUIPMENT

Metre ruler (yardstick) and pencil
Paper scissors
Quilter's rule
Tailor's chalk, fabric marker or quilter's crease
Fabric scissors
Rotary cutter and cutting mat
Sewing machine
Sewing needles and quilting needles
Iron and ironing board

MAKING THE TEMPLATES

To make the template for the bag sides, draw a 59 x 20-cm (23¼ x 8-in) rectangle on your paper. Cut out the template, fold it in half lengthwise, then mark the centre point along each long side. To make the template for the bag base, draw a circle with a 20-cm (8-in) diameter using a pair of compasses or by tracing around a small plate or bowl.

CUTTING OUT THE LINING FABRIC

One
For the strap, cut a strip 100-cm (39½-in) and 10-cm (4-in) wide across the width of the lining fabric.

Two
Using the templates, cut out one rectangle and two circles from the lining fabric.

MAKING THE PATCHWORK BAG

One
Start by making a small patchwork block from your fabric scraps. Take two fabric rectangles roughly the same size in any colours. With right sides together, join them along one side with a 1-cm (⅜-in) seam allowance. Don't cut the thread once the pieces have passed through the sewing machine, simply stitch on a little and line up two more pieces ready to be sewn.

Two
Repeat with more fabric scraps, sewing two pieces together at a time. Continue stitching until you have a long string of paired fabric pieces. Remove from the sewing machine and cut the threads to separate the pairs. Press all the seams open.

Three
With right sides together, sew two pairs along one side with a 1-cm (⅜-in) seam allowance. Using a quilter's rule and rotary cutter, trim the sides of the patch so that the two pairs sit flush, creating a new straight edge to grow your patchwork onto.

Four
Repeat step 3 to grow your patchwork, joining fabric pairs either at an angle (see page 87) or on a straight line to create a patchwork block. Play around with the composition and alternate the colours as you grow your block. Make enough blocks so that, when joined, they will be slightly larger than the rectangular template.

Five
Trim each block to straighten all the sides. With right sides together, join the blocks with a 1-cm (⅜-in) seam allowance to make one long length. Press all the seams open.

Six
Pin the rectangular template to the patchwork. Using a rotary cutter and cutting mat, trim around the template to neaten the edges. To stop the stitching from unravelling, sew a line of machine stitching 0.5 cm (¼ in) inside the outer edges.

Seven	Lay the wadding (batting) flat, centre the patchwork on top, then tack (baste) together to secure (see pages 38–40).
Eight	Stitch the patchwork and wadding (batting) with quilting stitches (see pages 30 and 34–35) as desired. Begin the stitching 1 cm (⅜ in) inside the edges so the stitches are not cut when making up the bag. Trim the wadding (batting) back to the size of the patchwork.
Nine	With right sides together, fold the patchwork in half lengthways. Mark the centre point on the fold along the bottom edge, then join the two short sides with a 1-cm (⅜-in) seam allowance.
Ten	Match up the side seam with the marked point on the opposite side of the patchwork piece. Mark the two new folds at the sides, again on the bottom edge. These marks will be used later to line up the bag base and sides.
Eleven	For the bag base, fold one circle of lining fabric in half and then in half again. Mark the point of all four folds.
Twelve	With right sides together, match the marks on the bag base with those on the outer bag and pin in place. Insert more pins all the way around the base to ensure a perfect fit. Sew around base with a 1-cm (⅜-in) seam allowance, making sure the fabric doesn't pucker. Turn the bag outer right side out and steam gently to press the seam.

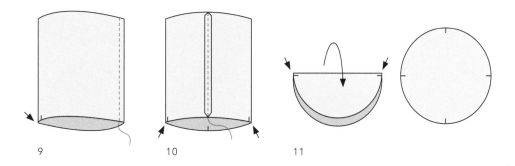

9   10   11

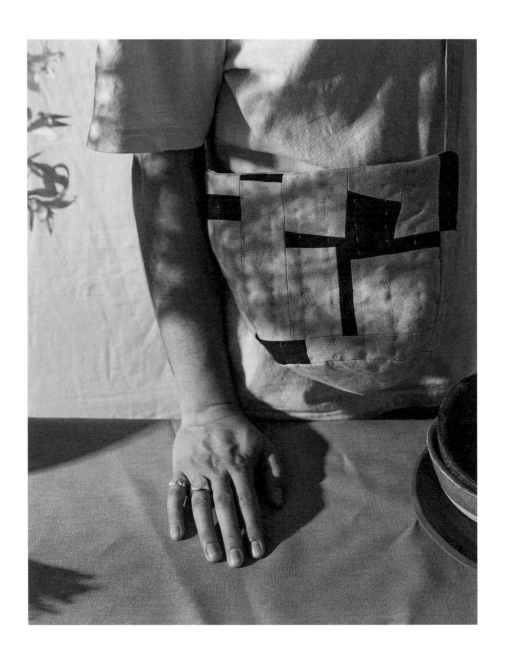

MAKING THE STRAP

One With wrong sides together, fold the strap in half lengthways. Press the fold. Open out the strap again, then fold both long sides into the centre to meet the fold line. Press again. Fold the strap in half again along the original fold to conceal the raw edges.

Two Sewing very close to the edge, stitch the strap closed along the long open side. Repeat on the opposite side of the strap. To strengthen the strap, work further lines of stitching down the length of the strap.

Three With right sides together, align one raw end of the strap to the top edge of the bag outer, then pin in place. Run the strap down and across the bag to the other side. Pin the other end of the strap to the opposite side of the bag outer, as before.

MAKING THE LINING

One Make the bag lining following steps 9–12 on page 93, but leaving a 7.5-cm (3-in) gap in the side seam that will be used later to turn the bag right side out once lined.

CONSTRUCTING THE BAG

One With right sides together, slide the bag outer inside the lining. The strap must sit between the bag outer and lining. Align the top edges and side seams, then stitch all the way around the opening with a 1-cm (⅜-in) seam allowance. Make sure the ends of the strap are stitched in the seam.

Two Pull the bag and strap through the gap in the lining so the bag is now right side out, the lining sits inside the bag and all seams are hidden. Press all edges.

Three Using matching thread, hand sew the gap in the lining closed with slip stitch (see page 35).

BROKEN LADDER QUILT

The Broken Ladder Quilt is created by combining informal strip blocks in various widths to create an interesting broken ladder pattern across the surface of the quilt. I have used two colours to accentuate the stripes and create a graphic statement quilt.

Size: 140 x 140 cm (55 x 55 in). You can adjust the finished size, but you will need to calculate the amount of fabric needed.

MATERIALS

Quilt top fabric: 100 cm (1⅛ yd) of 150-cm (59-in) wide cotton or linen in each of two colours.

Backing fabric: 150 cm (1¾ yd) of 150-cm (59-in) wide cotton or linen, or piece together smaller sections of fabric to create a backing at least 10 cm (4 in) wider and longer than the quilt top.

Wadding (batting): 145 x 145 cm (57 x 57 in), or at least 5 cm (2 in) wider and longer than the finished quilt.

Binding: At least 6.5 m (7⅛ yd) of 7.5-cm (3-in) wide straight binding in colour of your choice.

Sewing thread: Strong sewing thread.

Quilting thread: 10 g ball of pearl cotton crochet thread size 8 or similar in colour of your choice.

TOOLS AND EQUIPMENT

Fabric scissors
Rotary cutter and cutting mat
Sewing machine
Sewing needles and quilting needles
Iron and ironing board

QUILT PLAN

The Broken Ladder Quilt is made up of various sized stripe blocks. Those blocks are then joined together to create four larger strips, each the width of the final quilt measurement. As long as they add up to the length of the final quilt when joined, the four strips can each be a different depth for added visual interest.

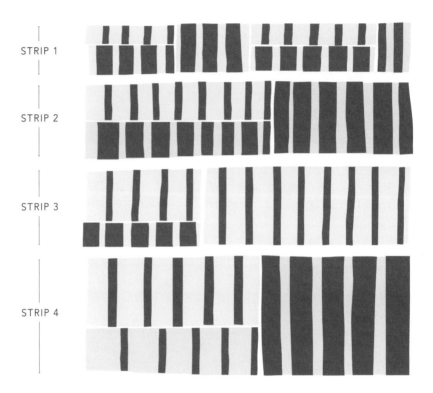

STRIP 1

STRIP 2

STRIP 3

STRIP 4

MAKING THE STRIP BLOCKS

One

Cut the two quilt top fabrics into four to give eight rectangles.

Two

Place a piece of each colour fabric together. Using a rotary cutter and cutting mat, cut both layers of fabric into strips of varying sizes. Take the first strip from the top layer and the second strip from the bottom layer. Join them together with a 1-cm (⅜-in) seam allowance. Next, add on the third strip from the top layer and then the fourth strip from the bottom layer. Continue in this way, alternating colours from the two layers to make the first length of strips. Repeat with the remaining strips to make a second length of strips, which mirrors the first.

Three	Continue to make more lengths of strips in alternating colours, varying the width of the strips and the length of the entire piece.
Four	Once all the strips have been joined into lengths, cut the lengths into smaller blocks. Lay out these smaller blocks into four long strips. To create the 'broken ladder' effect, place strips of contrasting colours next to each other – move the pieces around until you are happy with the size and composition. If preferred, use the quilt plan opposite as a guide.
Five	Once you are happy with the arrangement, join the lengths of strips with a 1-cm (⅜-in) seam allowance to form the larger strip blocks. Press all the seams open. Make sure that each strip block is at least 140 cm (55 in) long, or your chosen size.

ASSEMBLING THE QUILT TOP

One	Trim each block to straighten all the sides.
Two	With right sides together, join the blocks with a 1-cm (⅜-in) seam allowance to make up the quilt top in the desired size. Press all the seams open.

CONSTRUCTING AND FINISHING THE QUILT

One	Construct the quilt by assembling the layers (see page 38) and stitching with quilting stitches (see pages 30 and 34–35) as desired.
Two	Bind the edges of the quilt with the pre-prepared binding strip (see pages 42–49).

CIRCULAR CUSHION

I love to hand paint secondhand fabrics, which I then cut up and collage back together to create abstract patterns. This round cushion is a great way to use up those handpainted fabrics, at the same time playing around with colour and composition. If you don't want to paint fabrics yourself, use a selection of interesting prints – a large print will create a strong graphic design.

Size: 45 cm (17¾ in) in diameter.

MATERIALS

Cushion front fabric: 50 cm (20 in) of 122-cm (48-in) wide printed or patterned cotton or linen.

Backing fabric for the quilted cushion front: 50 x 50 cm (20 x 20 in) of lightweight cotton, such as cotton lawn or similar.

Wadding (batting): 50 x 50 cm (20 x 20 in).

Backing fabric for cushion: 50 cm (20 in) of 122-cm (48-in) wide lightweight cotton or linen in matching or contrasting colour.

Sewing thread: Strong sewing thread to match your chosen fabric.

Quilting thread: 10 g ball of pearl cotton crochet thread size 8 or similar in a colour of your choice.

46-cm (18-in) circular cushion pad.

Paper for template: 50 x 50-cm (20 x 20-in) piece of dot-and-cross pattern paper or brown parcel paper.

TOOLS AND EQUIPMENT

Metre ruler (yardstick) and pencil
Paper scissors
Quilter's rule
Tailor's chalk, fabric marker or quilter's crease
Fabric scissors
Rotary cutter and cutting mat
Sewing machine
Sewing needles and quilting needles
Iron and ironing board

MAKING THE TEMPLATE

To make the template for the cushion, draw a circle with a 46-cm (18-in) diameter using a pair of compasses or by tracing around a plate or bowl.

MAKING THE PATCHWORK CUSHION FRONT

One   Cut the cushion front fabric into 12 pieces, each measuring 10 x 26 cm (4 x 10¼ in).

Two   Lay out the pieces in four groups of three strips, making sure each grouping is different and any pattern on the original fabric is broken up.

Three   To make the first block, join the three strips with a 1-cm (⅜-in) seam allowance. Press the seams open. Repeat with the remaining strips to make three more square blocks.

2

3

Four   Arrange the blocks into a square. Lay the squares out so that the strips run horizontally in the top right and lower left corners, but vertically in the top left and lower right corners.

Five   With right sides together, join the top two blocks with a 1-cm (⅜-in) seam allowance. Repeat for the bottom two blocks.

Six   Join the two rectangles with a 1-cm (⅜-in) seam allowance to make a square measuring approximately 50 cm (19¾ in), taking care to line up the centre seams.

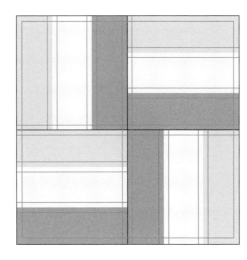

4–6

Seven	Fold the circular template in half and then in half again. Mark the point of all four folds. Unfold the circular template and place it on the centre of the patchwork piece, lining up the marked points with the main seams between each square block. Draw around the template.
Eight	Work a line of machine stitching 0.5 cm (¼ in) inside the drawn line to stabilise the patchwork, then cut out the circle along the line with fabric scissors.
Nine	Construct the cushion front by assembling the backing for the quilted cushion front, wadding (batting) and quilted cushion front layers (see pages 38) and stitching with quilting stitches (see pages 30 and 34–35) as desired. Begin and end the quilting stitches within the seam allowance. Trim away any excess wadding (batting) and backing.

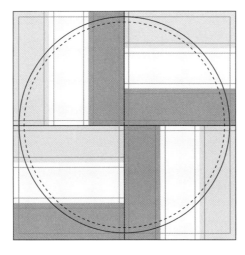

8

MAKING THE CUSHION BACK

One   Re-fold the circular template in half, then mark a line 10 cm (4 in) down from the centre fold. Cut along the drawn line.

Two   Using the adjusted circular template, cut out two identical cushion backs from the backing fabric.

Three   Press a 1-cm (⅜-in) double hem along the straight edges of both cushion back pieces, making sure the raw edges are hidden inside the folds. Using your sewing machine, topstitch along both hems.

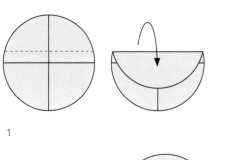

1

2

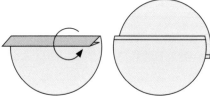

3

CONSTRUCTING THE CUSHION

One Lay the quilted cushion front out flat with the right side facing upwards. With right sides together, place the first cushion back panel over the cushion front, aligning the circular sides along the top edge.

Two With right sides together, place the second cushion back panel over the cushion front, aligning the circular sides along the bottom edge and overlapping the straight hemmed edges of both back panels across the centre of the cushion. Pin all the pieces in place.

Three Machine stitch all the way around the outside edge of the cushion, stitching 1-cm (⅜-in) in from the edge and working through all the layers.

Four Make small snips into the seam allowance all the way around the edge of the sewn cushion cover – this will help the seam to curve neatly once the cover is turned right side out.

Five Turn the cushion cover right side out. Insert the circular cushion pad through the envelope opening in the back panels.

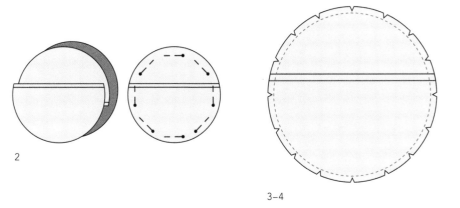

2

3–4

Tip Keep on gently pushing the cushion pad around the inside of your cushion cover until you get a nice round shape.

TAKEL ROLL

'Takel' in Cornish means tool. This practical roll can be used for a number of items: sewing tools, paintbrushes or even cutlery for a picnic. The Takel Roll is an easy project to make and can be created from either plain or patch-worked textiles.

Size: 50 x 35 cm (20 x 13¾ in) when unrolled.

MATERIALS

Fabric: 50 cm (20 in) of 150-cm (59-in) wide medium-weight cotton or linen in colour of your choice.

Wadding (batting): 50 x 35 cm (20 x 13¾ in).

Binding: At least 250 cm (2¼ yd) of 7.5-cm (3-in) wide straight binding in a colour of your choice.

Sewing thread: Strong sewing thread to match your chosen fabric.

Quilting thread: 10 g ball of pearl cotton crochet thread size 8 or similar in colour of your choice.

Paper for template: 50 x 50-cm (20 x 20-in) piece of dot-and-cross pattern paper or brown parcel paper.

TOOLS AND EQUIPMENT

Metre ruler (yardstick) and pencil
Paper scissors
Quilter's rule
Tailor's chalk, fabric marker or quilter's crease
Fabric scissors
Rotary cutter and cutting mat
Sewing machine
Sewing needles and quilting needles
Iron and ironing board

MAKING THE TEMPLATE

To make the template for the roll front and back, draw a 50 x 35-cm (20 x 13¾-in) rectangle on your paper. To make the template for the roll pocket, draw a 50 x 15-cm (20 x 6-in) rectangle on the remaining paper. Cut out the templates.

CUTTING OUT THE FABRIC PIECES

One — Using the templates for the roll front and back and the roll pocket, cut the fabric pieces from the full width of the fabric – cut two rectangles for the roll front and back and one rectangle for the roll pocket.

Two — From the remaining fabric, cut two strips from the full width, measuring 150 x 7.5 cm (59 x 3 in) for the binding.

Three — From the scrap of fabric left, cut two strips measuring 50 x 4 cm (20 x 1½ in) for the ties.

MAKING THE TAKEL ROLL

One — With the right side facing downwards, lay the roll back piece flat on your work surface. Place the wadding (batting) on top. Now lay the roll front piece over the wadding (batting) with right side facing upwards. Align all raw edges and tack (baste) the layers together with long stitches (see pages 38–40).

Two — Press a 1-cm (⅜-in) double hem along one long straight edge of the pocket piece, making sure the raw edge is hidden inside the folds. Using your sewing machine, topstitch along the hem.

Three — With the right side facing upwards, lay the pocket piece on top of the fabric and wadding (batting) layers, aligning the bottom edges and sides. Insert a few pins to hold the pocket piece in place, but do not add too many as you will lift the pocket in the next steps to quilt the lines that run through the main roll only.

Four — Turn the layered fabric 90 degrees clockwise so that one short edge is now facing you and the pocket piece is on the left side. Lift the first third of the pocket piece up and out of the way, removing any pins as necessary but keeping the pocket pinned in place further along. Mark a line 3 cm (1¼ in) in from the short edge.

Five — Working edge to edge, work quilting stitches (see pages 30 and 34–35) along the marked line.

Six	Lay the pocket flat again, aligning all raw edges. Mark a second line 2.5 cm (1 in) along from the first line, taking it across the roll and pocket this time. Work quilting stitches along this line, as before.
Seven	Lift the pocket down towards you and out of the way of the next line of stitching. Mark a third line 2.5 cm (1 in) along from the second line. Work quilting stitches along this line through the roll only, as before.
Eight	Repeat steps 6–7, sewing through the pocket on every other line of quilting stitches, until you reach the end of the roll.

ADDING THE TIES AND BINDING

One	Fold and press the tie pieces following the instructions given in step 1 of Making the strap on page 95.
Two	Fully open out one end of each tie, then fold a 1–2-cm (⅜–¾-in) hem to the wrong side to neaten. Re-fold along the original pressed lines, then stitch the ties following the instructions given in step 2 of Making the strap on page 95.
Three	Mark the centre point along one short side of the roll. With raw edges aligned, pin the two ties, side by side, at the marked centre point. The full length of the ties should lie over the roll – pin them to the roll to keep them out of the way while adding the binding.
Four	Bind the edges of the roll with the pre-prepared binding strip (see pages 42–49). When you reach the ties, stitch the binding over the raw ends to secure the ties in place.

Tip	When holding small items, fold the top edge of the roll down before rolling and tying to keep the objects in place. When holding larger items, like paintbrushes and tools, leave the roll unfolded.
	To secure the roll with the ties, wrap one clockwise and the other counterclockwise around the roll a few times, then tie together.

FESTIVAL POUCH

The Festival Pouch was inspired by my first-ever festival experience at Port Eliot in Cornwall. It is the perfect size to hold all of your essentials in for the day, while still being able to enjoy the festivities and dance around late into the evening. You can use any patchwork or appliqué techniques from the workshops in this book to create your own design and then the bag can either be quilted or left plain.

Size: 22 x 18 cm (9 x 7 in) excluding strap.

MATERIALS

Outer bag fabric: Enough scraps or remnants of cotton or linen to make a 46 x 20-cm (18 x 8-in) patchwork rectangle.

Bag lining fabric: 44 x 18 cm (17¼ x 7 in) of lightweight cotton fabric, such as cotton lawn or similar.

Wadding (batting) (optional): 44 x 18 cm (17¼ x 7 in), if quilting the pouch.

Strap fabric: Enough remnants of cotton or linen to make a 160 x 6-cm (63 x 2⅜-in) strip.

Sewing thread: Strong sewing thread in matching or contrasting colour to the fabric.

Quilting thread: 10 g ball of pearl cotton crochet thread size 8 or similar in colour of your choice.

TOOLS AND EQUIPMENT

Fabric scissors
Rotary cutter and cutting mat
Quilter's rule
Tailor's chalk, fabric marker or quilter's crease
Sewing machine
Sewing needles and quilting needles
Iron and ironing board

CUTTING OUT THE STRAPS

One   Fold the fabric in half widthways, from selvedge to selvedge. Cut two strips, each 6 cm (2⅜ in) wide across the full width of the fabric.

MAKING THE BAG

One   Using any of the techniques outlined in Workshop Three (see page 54–63), join your selection of fabrics into a patchwork block measuring 46 x 20 cm (18 x 8 in).

Two   With right sides together, pin the bag lining piece to the patchwork bag outer piece, making sure the lining is centred. Sew along both short sides with a 1-cm (⅜-in) seam allowance. Trim any excess fabric from the bag outer in line with the lining. Press the seam open. Turn right sides out and press again.

Three   Slide the wadding (batting) between the bag outer and lining, making sure the wadding (batting) is flat and the sides align with the pressed seams.

Four   Fold all the layers in half widthways and lightly press the fold. Unfold and then machine stitch down the fold line to secure the layers through the centre.

Five   If you are quilting your pouch, work the quilting stitches (see pages 30 and 34–35) using straight lines, curved lines or other shapes.

Six   Fold the joined layers in half again with the patchwork bag outer on the outside and the lining on the inside. Insert pins down the open edge to hold in place.

ADDING THE STRAP

One Join the two bag strap pieces into one long strip with a 1-cm (⅜-in) seam allowance following the instructions given in steps 3–5 on page 42. Press the seam open. Trim the strap down to 160 cm (63 in).

Two Fold and press the strap following the instructions given in step 1 of Making the strap on page 95.

Three Fully open out both ends of the strap, then fold 2-cm (¾-in) hems to the wrong side to neaten. Measure and mark 4 cm (1⅝ in) in from each folded edge.

Four With right sides together and lining up the marked line on the strap with the bottom edge of the bag, place one long raw edge of the opened-out strap against the side seam of the bag and pin in place.

Five Making sure that the strap is not twisted at any point, take the rest of the strap around to the other folded side of the bag and pin the strap in place as before.

Six Using the crease of the fold line as a guide, stitch the strap in place down the length of the bag on both sides.

Seven Re-fold the strap over to enclose the sides of the bag. The long folded edge of the strap should just cover the stitch line on the reverse of the bag. If necessary, trim back the outer bag seam allowance to 0.5cm (¼ in), keeping the strap out of the way. Tack (baste) (see page 40) the strap in place.

Eight Starting at the bottom edge of one side of the bag, stitch all the way along the open side of the strap to the opposite side of the bag and continue down to the other bottom edge. All raw edges of the bag should now be enclosed.

Tip Machine stitching a narrow strap closed can sometimes be tricky. If preferred, hand stitch the strap closed with a slip stitch (see page 35) for a neat finish.

Add a press stud inside the top of the bag to keep it closed, for extra security.

SCENTED SACHET

The Scented Sachet is simple to make and is perfect for adding to drawers
or hanging up in wardrobes to fragrance your belonging and ward away insects.
It can even be carried in your bags or pockets. This is a great project to use
up any fabric scraps as the sachet can be made in any size or shape. Scent the
sachet using essentials oils. Use a slightly open weave or thinner fabric for
the backing so the essential oils will penetrate the cloth and the filling inside.

Size: 8 x 8 cm (3¼ x 3¼ in). You can adjust
the finished size, but you will need to calculate
the amount of fabric needed.

MATERIALS

Front and backing fabric: Two 10-cm (4-in)
squares of loose-weave cotton, linen
or cheesecloth.

Hanging loop: 10 x 4 cm (4 x 1⅝ in) cotton
or linen, or 10 cm (4 in) of 2.5-cm (1-in)
wide ribbon.

Wadding (batting): 10-cm (4-in) square for the
sachet, plus offcuts and scraps for the filling.

Sewing thread: Strong sewing thread in
matching or contrasting colour to the fabric.

Quilting thread: 10 g ball of pearl cotton
crochet thread size 8 or similar in colour
of your choice.

TOOLS AND EQUIPMENT

Fabric scissors
Rotary cutter and cutting mat
Quilter's rule
Tailor's chalk, fabric marker or quilter's crease
Sewing machine
Sewing needles and quilting needles
Iron and ironing board

MAKING THE SACHET

One — Decide on the size and shape of your sachet and cut your fabric and wadding (batting) to size – you need two pieces of fabric for the sachet front and back and one piece of wadding (batting). The one shown here was made from 10-cm (4-in) squares.

Two — If quilting the sachet front, lay the front piece on top of the wadding (batting) and pin in place. For my quilted sachet, I worked straight parallel lines of quilting stitches (see pages 30 and 34–35) spaced 1.5 cm (⅝ in) apart across the layers. I then turned the piece 90 degrees and worked more straight lines so that they formed a check pattern.

Three — If making the hanging loop from fabric, fold and stitch the loop following the instructions in steps 1–3 of Adding a hanging sleeve on page 129.

Four — Fold the hanging loop in half and place it on the right side of the quilted piece, in the middle of one side, with the ends of the loop aligned with the raw edge and the loop pointing into the centre of the sachet. Lay the backing fabric on top. The loop is now enclosed in the layers.

Five — Starting just before the loop, stitch all the way around the outer edge with a 1-cm (⅜-in) seam allowance but leaving a 4-cm (1⅝-in) gap.

Six — Turn the sachet right side out through the gap in the seam.

Seven — Stuff the sachet with small scraps of wadding (batting) until it is plump. Do not overstuff or it will be difficult to sew closed.

Eight — Tuck the seam allowances inside along the gap. Using a matching sewing thread, slip stitch (see page 35) the gap closed.

ADDING A SCENT TO THE SACHET

Add a few drops of essential oils to the back of your sachet.

Relax and unwind: 2 drops Sweet Marjoram, 2 drops Chamomile. Chamomile was used in ancient herbal medicines to reduce levels of stress and anxiety. Sweet marjoram is known for its calming qualities.

Re-energise: 3 drops Grapefruit, 2 drops Peppermint, 1 drop Spearmint. Grapefruit is zesty, bright and uplifting. It has the power to balance mood and emotions while elevating spirits. Peppermint is effective for preventing fatigue and improving exercise performance. Spearmint encourages a sense of focus while also uplifting mood.

Keeping bugs at bay: 2 drops Tea Tree, 2 drops Lemongrass, 2 drops Orange. This is a great recipe for when you're out and about. Tea tree is effective against mosquitoes, bush flies and biting midges. Lemongrass helps to repel mosquitoes, fleas, fruit flies and moths. Orange is especially effective at keeping ants away, as well as other insects such as crickets and spiders.

Tip

You can make these sachets any size and shape and also with different stitching techniques. For my round sachet, I appliquéd small shapes across the top layer instead of quilting it. Draw a circle onto a larger piece of cloth, and then apply appliqué shapes. Stitch the shapes down, but if they overlap the drawn line only stitch within the line to avoid cutting through the stitching when the excess appliqué is cut away. Follow the same instructions as for the square sachet to complete your sachet.

LOER WALLHANGING

'Loer' is the Cornish word for moon. This patchwork wallhanging
with its attractive curves is created from a repeating half-moon pattern,
using an alternating colour palette.

Size: 80 x 120 cm (31½ x 47¼ in). You can adjust
the finished size, but you will need to calculate
the amount of fabric needed.

MATERIALS

Quilt top fabric: 30 cm (12 in) of 150-cm (59-in)
wide cotton or linen in each of four colours.

Backing fabric: 90 x 130 cm (35½ x 51¼ in)
of cotton or linen, or piece together smaller
sections of fabric to create a backing at least
10 cm (4 in) wider and longer than the quilt top.

Wadding (batting): 85 x 125 cm (33½ x 49¼ in),
or at least 5 cm (2 in) wider and longer than
the quilt top.

Binding: At least 4.6 m (5 yd) of 7.5-cm (3-in)
wide binding.

Sewing thread: Strong sewing thread in
matching or contrasting colour to the fabric.

Quilting thread: 10 g ball of pearl cotton crochet
thread size 8 or similar in colour of your choice.

Paper for template: 25 x 45-cm (10 x 17¾-in)
piece of dot-and-cross pattern paper
or brown parcel paper.

TOOLS AND EQUIPMENT

Metre ruler (yardstick) and pencil
Paper scissors
Quilter's rule
Tailor's chalk, fabric marker or quilter's crease
Fabric scissors
Rotary cutter and cutting mat
Sewing machine
Sewing needles and quilting needles
Iron and ironing board

MAKING THE TEMPLATE

This quilted wallhanging is formed of twelve half-moon blocks, each with a finished size of 20 x 40 cm (8 x 16 in). Four blocks are stitched together in rows and then the three rows are joined to create the final quilt top, lining up the seams as you go.

To make the template for the patchwork block, draw a 22 x 44-cm (8⅝ x 17¼-in) rectangle on your paper. Cut out the template. This template will be used later to trim the blocks to size after they have been pieced together. (Some fabric will be lost in the curved seams.)

MAKING THE PANELS

One

Divide the four quilt top fabrics into three equal panels. From 150-cm (59-in) wide fabric, you should get three 30 x 50-cm (12 x 20-in) panels from each fabric, giving you a total of 12 panels. If you are using remnants, make sure you have 12 panels in four different colours.

Two

With right sides facing upwards, layer two panels in different colours on top of each other on the cutting mat. Measure and mark at least 5 cm (2 in) in from the top and bottom edges of the panel on the right-hand side. This is where the curve will start and finish.

Three

Using the rotary cutter, firmly cut a half-moon shape freehand through both layers, starting at one of the marks and ending at the other. The apex of the moon should roughly end up in the middle of the two marks.

Four

Separate the blocks and pair each half-moon shape with a contrast-colour border. Fit the half-moons into place on both panels with curved edges touching. Make horizontal marks on both sides of each half-moon to act as matching up points when sewing the pieces together.

Five

To join the first panel, place the half-moon and border with right sides together, matching the marks. Pin together all along the curve.

Six

With the half-moon on the bottom and the border on the top, stitch the two pieces together around the curve with a 0.5-cm (¼-in) seam allowance. To avoid puckers, work slowly and make sure the curved seam sits evenly. Check which side the seam naturally wants to curve towards and press it to that side. Turn the panel over and press it again to smooth out the seam.

Seven	Place the panel on the cutting mat with the template on top, lining it up so that the apex of the curve sits within the middle or two-thirds of the way inside the template – you don't want to cut off the top of the curve or lose it in a seam. Trim around all four sides of the template with the rotary cutter to create a neat 22 x 42-cm (8⅝ x 17¼-in) block.
Eight	Repeat steps 2–7 until you have 12 blocks, pieced and trimmed, alternating colours for a good mix of colour combinations.

ASSEMBLING THE QUILT TOP

One	Arrange the blocks into three rows of four, making sure none of the same colours are touching, and that the same colour combinations are not too close to each other.
Two	Once you are happy with the composition, sew the blocks into rows and then the rows into the quilt top with a 1-cm (⅜-in) seam allowance, taking care to line up the vertical and horizontal seams across all the strips. Turn the quilt top over and give it a final press to neaten.

CONSTRUCTING AND FINISHING THE WALLHANGING

One	Construct the wallhanging by assembling the layers (see pages 38–41) and stitching with quilting stitches (see pages 30 and 34–35) as desired.
Two	Bind the edges of the wallhanging with the pre-prepared binding strip (see pages 42–49).

ADDING A HANGING SLEEVE

One	Cut a strip of fabric measuring 23 cm (9 in) wide and as long as the width of the wallhanging plus 4 cm (1½ in).
Two	Press a 1-cm (⅜-in) double hem along both short ends, making sure the raw edges are hidden inside the folds. Using your sewing machine, topstitch along both hems.
Three	With wrong sides together, fold the strip in half lengthwise with raw edges touching. Press the edges.
Four	Open the strip out, then fold the top and bottom edges inot the centrefold created in step 3. Press the edges.
Five	With top and bottom edges aligned, sew them together with a 1-cm (⅜-in) seam allowance. This creates a fold or hanging sleeve to accomodate the dowel.
Six	Place the sleeve on the backing of the wallhanging, seam side down with the top edge lined up with the top edge of the wallhanging. Bring the sleeve down from the top edge of the wallhanging by about 3.75 cm (1½ in), so that when hung the sleeve and dowel don't show above the top of the wallhanging.
Seven	Pin in place and then sew the top edge of the sleeve to the backing of the wallhanging with a whip stitch (see page 34). Do not stitch through the quilt front.
Eight	Repeat on the lower edge of the sleeve.
Nine	Finally, whip stitch across the two short ends only where they touch the back of the quilt, leaving the ends of the sleeve open.
Ten	Using a hacksaw, cut a length of dowel so that it is slightly longer than the hanging sleeve and slightly shorter than the quilt. Thread the dowel through the sleeve so the ends protrude at each end, but they do not show from the front.
Eleven	Tie a length of hanging cord to each end of the dowel and hang the wallhanging like a picture. Alternatively, fix a pair of nails or screws into the wall positioned so you can hook the ends of the dowels over them.

Tip	If you want to use this piece as a regular quilt after you have used it as a wallhanging, then remove the sleeve by unpicking the stitches holding it in place.

TEXTILE COLLAGE

In the studio I make small textile studies to experiment with colour and shapes. They are quick to make and a great way to trial compositions when designing a larger quilt. They also make really lovely objects to put in antique frames.

Size: Can be adjusted to fit any size picture frame.

MATERIALS

Fabric: Selection of remnants or offcuts of any fabric in an assortment of colours left over from other projects.

Backing fabric: A length of fabric or small scraps pieced together to make a piece the same size as the finished textile collage.

Wadding (batting): A piece of wadding the same size as the finished textile collage.

Sewing thread: Strong sewing thread in matching or contrasting colour to the fabric.

Quilting thread: 10 g ball of pearl cotton crochet thread size 8 or similar in colour of your choice.

Picture frame in the size and style of your choice. Mount board cut to fit your chosen picture frame.

TOOLS AND EQUIPMENT

Fabric scissors
Rotary cutter and cutting mat
Sewing machine
Sewing needles and quilting needles
Iron and ironing board
Double-sided sticky tape

MAKING THE COLLAGE

One   Lay a selection of fabric scraps out on your work surface. Without overthinking it, take two fabric scraps in any colour. Do not worry if they aren't exactly the same size, if they don't fit together perfectly or if they don't have straight edges. With right sides together, join them along one side with a 1-cm (⅜-in) seam allowance. Trim any excess fabric from the seam allowance to create a straight edge. Press the seam open.

Two   Take another fabric scrap in any colour. Place it over the newly joined pieces and choose a side to stitch down. With right sides together, join them along one side with a 1-cm (⅜-in) seam allowance. Trim any excess fabric from the seam allowance to create a straight edge. Press the seam open.

Three   Repeat step 2 to add more fabric scraps, building up a random patchwork pattern, until you are happy with the composition. As the block gets bigger, experiment with different ways of adding fabric. Here are four suggestions:

x Cut a fabric scrap into three, jumble them up and then sew them back together.
x Cut a fabric scrap through the middle and insert a longer piece of fabric into the seam.
x Cut the fabric scrap apart with a curve and insert a new section using the curved patchwork technique on pages 57–58.
x Appliqué different fabric shapes onto the surface of your collage.

ASSEMBLING THE COLLAGE

One   Construct the collage by assembling the layers (see pages 38–41), tacking (basting) them together and stitching with quilting stitches (see pages 30 and 34–35) as desired. Experiment with different stitches in any configuration to create a collage personal to you.

Two   Trim the backing fabric and wadding (batting) to the size of the final patchwork textile collage.

Three   Using double-sided sticky tape, fix the back of the collage to the mount board to hold it in position. Before sticking the strips of tape to the board, check that the collage sits in the desired position within the frame. Place the mount board in the frame ready for display.

MOOR STONE CUSHION

The Moor Stone Cushion takes its curved abstract design from the undulating granite stones of the Cornish moor. Dotted across the landscape, these stones are sculptural monoliths rising up from the ground. This cushion plays with simple bold lines by using a patchwork of curved blocks in three colours, utilising the curved patchwork techniques on pages 57–61.

Size: 55 x 55 cm (21½ x 21½ in).

MATERIALS

Cushion front fabric: Approx. 30–40 cm (12–15¾ in) of 150-cm (59-in) wide cotton or linen in each of three colours.

Backing fabric for quilted cushion front: 66 x 66 cm (26 x 26 in) of lightweight cotton or linen, such as cotton lawn or similar.

Wadding (batting): 61 x 61 cm (24 x 24 in).

Backing fabric for cushion: Two 56 x 36-cm (22 x 10¾-in) rectangles of lightweight cotton or linen in matching or contrasting colour.

Binding: At least 3 m (3¼ yd) of 7.5-cm (3-in) wide straight binding in colour of your choice (see pages 42–49).

Sewing thread: Strong sewing thread to match your chosen fabric.

Quilting thread: 10 g ball of pearl cotton crochet thread size 8 or similar in colour of your choice.

55 cm (21¾ in) square cushion pad.

Paper for templates: 56 x 56-cm (22 x 22-in) piece of dot-and-cross pattern paper or brown parcel paper.

TOOLS AND EQUIPMENT

Metre ruler (yardstick) and pencil
Paper scissors
Quilter's rule
Tailor's chalk, fabric marker or quilter's crease
Fabric scissors
Rotary cutter and cutting mat
Sewing machine
Sewing needles and quilting needles
Iron and ironing board

MAKING THE TEMPLATE

To make the template for the cushion front, cut out a 56-cm (22-in) square from the paper.

The design for this cushion front is centered around four curved patchwork blocks, which are then pieced together with infill sections of fabric to create the final composition. By limiting your palette to just three colours, graphic shapes and clear lines will form.

MAKING THE PATCHWORK CUSHION FRONT

One

Using each of the fabrics in three different colours, create four curved patchwork blocks in varying sizes following the instructions on pages 57–58. The four curved patchwork blocks should more or less cover the surface area of the cushion front template, but without overlapping. As a guide, the blocks in the cushion shown here measure (including seam allowances):

Block 1: 32 x 37 cm (12½ x 14½ in)
Block 2: 32 x 27 cm (12½ x 10½ in)
Block 3: 22 x 37 cm (8¾ x 14½ in)
Block 4: 22 x 17 cm (8¾ x 6¾ in)

Trim the sides of the four curved patchwork blocks to give straight edges on which to join on the smaller infill pieces of fabric in step 4.

Two

Lay the four curved patchwork blocks over the cushion front template. Play around with the placement of the blocks until you are happy with the composition and they cover the template.

Three

Measure the negative spaces between the curved patchwork blocks to calculate how much additional fabric you need for the infill pieces to join the blocks together. Cut the infill pieces from the leftover cushion front fabric to roughly the correct size – you can either trim the infill pieces down to the exact size after stitching or before inserting them.

Four

Following your chosen composition, join together the curved patchwork blocks and infill pieces with right sides together and 1-cm (⅜-in) seam allowances. Press all seams open as you sew.

Five

Lay the cushion front template over the top of the patchwork cushion front, centering it over the design, and pin it in place. Draw around the template.

Six	Remove the template. Work a line of machine stitching 0.5 cm (¼ in) inside the drawn lines all around the cushion front to stabilise the patchwork, then cut out the square along the lines with fabric scissors.
Seven	Construct the cushion front by assembling the backing for the quilted cushion front, wadding (batting) and quilted cushion front layers (see page 38) and stitching with quilting stitches (see pages 30 and 34–35) as desired. (I spaced my lines of quilting stitches 2.5 cm/I in apart across the entire cushion front.) Begin and end the quilting stitches within the seam allowance. Trim away any excess wadding (batting) and backing.

MAKING THE CUSHION BACK

One	Press a I-cm (⅜-in) double hem along the straight edges of both cushion back pieces, turning the hems to either the wrong side or right side and making sure the raw edges are hidden inside the folds. Using your sewing machine, topstitch along both hems.

CONSTRUCTING THE CUSHION

One   Lay the quilted cushion front out flat with the right side facing downwards. With wrong sides together, place the first cushion back panel over the cushion front, aligning the raw edges along the bottom and side edges.

Two   With wrong sides together, place the second cushion back panel over the cushion front, aligning the raw edges along the top and side edges and overlapping the straight hemmed edges of both back panels across the centre of the cushion. Pin all the pieces in place.

Three   Tack (baste) the cushion pieces together around the edges, working through all the layers. Now tack (baste) the back panels together across the envelope opening to keep them in place while adding the binding.

Four   Bind the edges of the cushion with the pre-prepared binding strip (see pages 42–49).

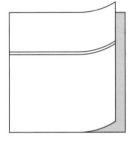

1—2

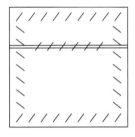

3

RITUALS CUSHION

The Rituals Cushion is designed for lazy days, time spent by yourself for much-needed moments of rest. A large floor cushion created using the wholecloth quilting method with intersecting lines of stitches that make a check pattern, it's the perfect project to make something luxurious for yourself.

Size: 81 x 81 cm (32 x 32 in).

MATERIALS

Cushion front and envelope back: 135 cm (53¼ in) of 150-cm (59-in) wide cotton or linen.

Backing fabric for quilted cushion front: 91 x 91 cm (36 x 36 in) lightweight cotton or linen, such as cotton lawn.

Wadding (batting): Approx 86 x 86 cm (34 x 34 in).

Binding: At least 4 m (4⅜ yd) of 7.5-cm (3-in) wide straight binding in a contrasting colour to the cushion (see pages 42–49).

Sewing thread: Strong sewing thread to match your chosen fabric.

Quilting thread: 10 g ball of pearl cotton crochet thread size 8 or similar in colour of your choice.

81-cm (32-in) square cushion pad.

TOOLS AND EQUIPMENT

Metre ruler (yardstick) or quilter's rule
Tailor's chalk, fabric marker or quilter's crease
Fabric scissors
Rotary cutter and cutting mat
Sewing machine
Sewing needles and quilting needles
Iron and ironing board

CUTTING THE CUSHION FRONT AND BACKS

As a guide, the blocks in the cushion shown here measure (including seam allowances):

Cushion front – one 81 x 81-cm (32 x 32-in) square
Cushion backs – two 81 x 52-cm (32 x 20½-in) rectangles

MAKING THE QUILTED CUSHION FRONT

One — Press the backing fabric for the quilted cushion front (not the fabric for the envelope cushion back).

Two — Tape the pressed backing fabric to your work surface and centre the wadding (batting) on top. Lay the cushion front over the wadding with the right side facing upwards. Keep the edges of all the layers straight and even, checking with a ruler if necessary.

Three — Tack (baste) the cushion front pieces together around the edges, working through all the layers (see page 40).

Four — Measure and mark a line 5 cm (2 in) in from one edge of the cushion front. Cut a length of quilting thread that is slightly longer than the edge of the cushion. Using this thread, work a line of quilting stitches along the drawn line (see pages 30 and 34–35). Begin and end the quilting stitches within the seam allowance.

Five — Measure and mark another line 5 cm (2 in) along from the first stitched line. Work a line of quilting stitches along the drawn line, as before. Repeat until you have worked lines of quilting stitches across the entire cushion front.

Six — Return to the first and second lines of quilting stitches and draw another line spaced evenly between the two. Work a line of quilting stitches along this drawn line. Repeat between the third and fourth lines of quilting stitches and then between every other pair of stitched lines until you have worked across the entire cushion front. At this stage, you should have a 5-cm (2-in) gap followed by three lines of stitching, another 5-cm (2-in) gap and then another three lines of stitching, which is repeated across the piece.

Seven — Turn the cushion front 90 degrees ready to work further lines of stitching to make the check pattern. Repeat steps 4–6 to create a grid of quilting stitches that run perpendicular to each other.

CONSTRUCTING THE CUSHION

One — To make the cushion back and construct the cushion, including binding the edges, follow the instructions on pages 137–138.

WHEAT BAG

The warmth of a wheat bag can keep you cosy in winter or relieve the aches and pains of a long week. You can even add a few drops of essential oil for an extra soothing touch. For the two wheat bags shown here, I used a combination of straight and curved patchwork piecing, but you can use any of the techniques from the workshops in this book. The wheat bag is made up of an inner lining – which can be replaced –that holds the filling and an outer cover.

Size: 33 x 15 cm (13 x 6 in).

MATERIALS

Cover fabric: Selection of scraps or remnants of 100% cotton or linen in two or more contrasting colours to make two patchwork blocks that are just slightly larger than 35 x 17 cm (13¾ x 6¾ in).

Lining fabric: 50 x 50 cm (19¾ x 19¾ in) of lightweight 100% cotton calico.

Sewing thread: Strong sewing thread to match your chosen fabric.

Filling: 500 g (18 oz) of wheat berries, pearl barley or uncooked rice. Dried lavender or lavender essential oil or any essential oil of your choice (optional).

Paper for template: 35 x 17-cm (13¾ x 6¾-in) piece of dot-and-cross pattern paper or brown parcel paper.

TOOLS AND EQUIPMENT

Ruler and pencil
Paper scissors
Quilter's rule
Tailor's chalk, fabric marker or quilter's crease
Fabric scissors
Rotary cutter and cutting mat
Sewing machine
Sewing needles and quilting needles
Iron and ironing board

MAKING THE TEMPLATE

To make the template for the bag cover, cut out a 35 x 17-cm (13¾ x 6¾-in) rectangle from the paper.

MAKING THE BAG COVER

One | Using your fabric scraps and remnants, sew two patchwork blocks measuring just slightly larger than 35 x 17 cm (13¾ x 6¾ in) for the bag cover utilising any of the patchwork techniques from Workshop Three (see pages 54–63). Before piecing, arrange the fabric scraps on the template until you are happy with the composition. Stitch the patchwork blocks together using any of the techniques from the workshops at the beginning of this book.

Two | Lay the template over one of the patchwork blocks, centering it over the design, and pin it in place. Draw around the template. Remove the template. Repeat for the second patchwork block.

Three | Work a line of machine stitching 0.5 cm (¼ in) inside the drawn lines all around each block to stabilise the patchwork, then cut out the rectangles along the lines with fabric scissors.

Four | To join the two patchwork blocks, with right sides together and raw edges aligned, stitch all the way around the outer edge with a 1-cm (⅜-in) seam allowance but leaving a 10-cm (4-in) gap along one side. Turn the bag cover right side through the gap in the seam. Tuck the seam allowances inside along the gap and press to neaten.

MAKING THE LINING BAG

One	Using the template, cut two rectangles of cotton calico.
Two	Follow step 4 opposite to join the two panels, but leaving a small gap in one of the shortest side seams. With the lining bag right side out, fold the bag in half and mark the centre point along both long sides.
Three	If you want to add a scent to your wheat bag, pour the filling into a bowl and add either some dried lavender flowers or a few drops of your favourite essential oil and stir to mix.
Four	Using a funnel or a rolled-up cone of paper, pour half the filling into the lining bag to fill the lower half.
Five	Sew a line of stitching across the lining bag between the two marked centre points, working a few backstitches at each end, to keep the filling evenly distributed within the bag.
Six	Use the funnel or paper cone to fill the upper half of the lining bag with the remaining filling.
Seven	To close the lining bag, tuck the seam allowances inside along the gap and, using matching sewing thread, slip stitch (see page 35) the gap closed. Alternatively, machine stitch the gap closed, working a few backstitches at each end to secure the stitches.
Eight	Slip the filled lining bag inside the outer bag cover. Tuck inside the seam allowances of the outer bag along the gap and then, using matching sewing thread, slip stitch (see page 35) the gap closed.

Tip	To stop the wheat bag from burning or even catching alight, or damaging your microwave, place a mug of water in the microwave alongside the wheat bag when heating. When heating a wheat bag, only run the microwave for 30 seconds at a time on a low heat setting, checking the bag at regular intervals to make sure it does not scorch. Different fillings take more or less time to heat up. To cool the bag down, pop it inside a freezer bag and place it in the freezer for 2–3 hours. Do not use the wheat bag in bed or leave it unattended on soft furnishings.

SCULPTURAL WALLHANGING

The Sculptural Wallhanging takes its name from its composition of structural shapes that play off of each other's lines and curves. By balancing and leaning appliquéd shapes against one another, you can create sculptural designs on your quilt projects. The self-bound edge means there is no need for additional binding fabric.

Size: 60 x 80 cm (23½ x 31½ in). You can adjust the finished size, but you will need to calculate the amount of fabric needed.

MATERIALS

Wallhanging front: 60 x 80 cm (23½ x 31½ in) of cotton or linen.

Appliqué: Selection of scraps or remnants of cotton or linen in different colours.

Backing: 70 x 90 cm (27½ x 35½ in) of cotton or linen, or piece together smaller sections of fabric to create a backing at least 10 cm (4 in) wider and longer than the wallhanging front.

Wadding (batting): 65 x 85 cm (25½ x 33½ in), or at least 5 cm wider and longer than the wallhanging front.

Sewing thread: Strong sewing thread in matching or contrasting colour to the fabric.

Quilting thread: 10 g ball of pearl cotton crochet thread size 8 or similar in colour of your choice.

TOOLS AND EQUIPMENT

Metre ruler (yardstick) and pencil
Freezer paper
Paper scissors
Quilter's rule
Tailor's chalk, fabric marker or quilter's crease
Fabric scissors
Rotary cutter and cutting mat
Sewing machine
Sewing needles and quilting needles
Iron and ironing board

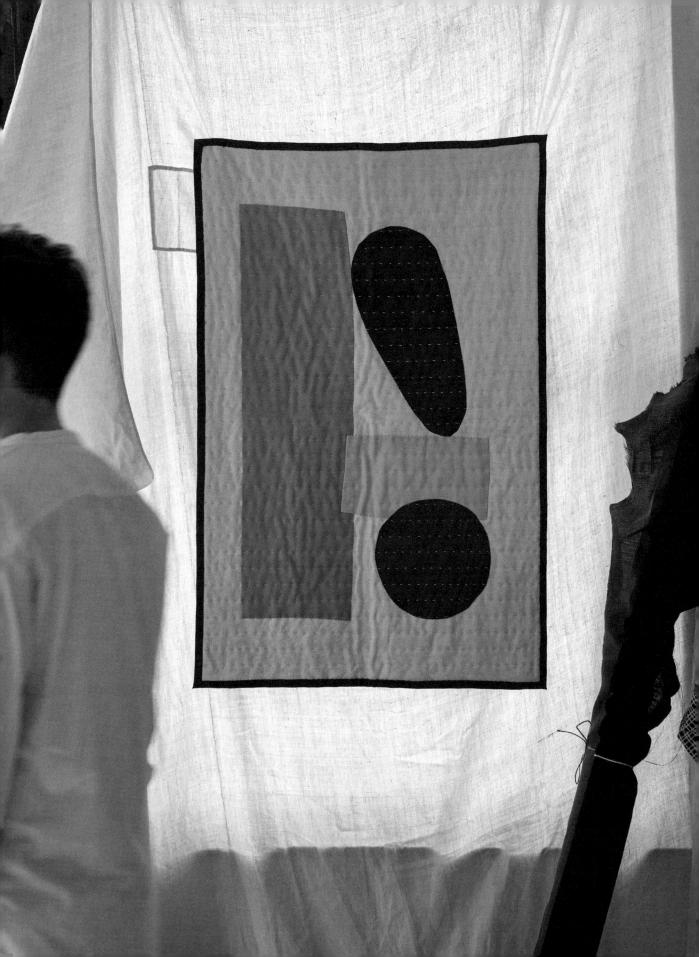

When making any simple quilted piece that incorporates appliqué, I prefer to construct the layers – but not quilt them – before adding the appliquéd shapes. I find this provides a more stable backing on which to sew when applying the appliqué. It also means that you can rework the design multiple times by arranging and re-arranging the appliqué shapes on the background until you are happy with the composition, so that you can see the design come together.

CONSTRUCTING THE WALLHANGING

One   Making sure that all edges are straight and even, layer the backing fabric, wadding (batting) and wallhanging front on top of each other, centering each piece and ensuring that there is an even border of backing fabric around each edge. Tack (baste) all of the layers together (see pages 38–41).

MAKING AND ATTACHING THE APPLIQUÉ SHAPES

One   Draw a selection of geometric shapes on to the matt side of the freezer paper. You can either draw the shapes freehand or use a ruler or trace around objects. Cut out the paper shapes.

Two   Choose which fabric you are using for each of the different shapes. Following the instructions on pages 66–67, make up the appliqué pieces. Remember to clip into any curves so that the fabric sits flat and the curves are smooth.

Three   Arrange the appliqué shapes across the right side of the wallhanging front. Take time over your composition, because now is your opportunity to move things around and play with the juxtaposing shapes. Lean curves against straight lines or balance straight lines on top of curves until your sculpture comes to life.

Four   When you are happy with the composition, tack (baste) all of the appliqué shapes in place to prevent them moving around.

Five   Following the instructions on page 68, sew the appliqué shapes to the wallhanging front using invisible stitching.

FINISHING THE WALLHANGING

One — Quilt the wallhanging in any way that you like – I quilted simple straight lines to let the geometric shapes of the appliqué stand out, but you could follow the lines of your shapes, or quilt each shape individually to create a different effect. See pages 30 and 34–35 for detailed instructions on quilting.

Two — Self-bind the edges of the wallhanging following the instructions on page 51.

Three — Add the hanging sleeve following the instructions on page 129.

BABAN QUILT

'Baban' is the Cornish word for baby and this little quilt is a playful project for the little people in our lives. As soon as I grew out of them, most of my childhood things were handed down to the next generation. With that in mind, I designed this quilt – made up of separate blocks, each decorated with appliqué, that are then stitched together – to be a colourful heirloom. To create a truly memorable quilt that brings the whole family together, ask individual members to each complete a block.

Size: 100 x 100 cm (39⅜ x 39⅜ in). You can adjust the finished size, but you will need to calculate the amount of fabric needed.

MATERIALS

Patchwork blocks: 75 cm (29½ in) of 150-cm (59-in) wide cotton or linen, or enough offcuts or remnants to give sixteen 24 x 24-cm (9½ x 9½-in) squares.

Appliqué: Selection of scraps or remnants of cotton or linen in different colours.

Backing: 110 x 110 cm (43⅜ x 43⅜ in) of cotton or linen, or piece together smaller sections of fabric to create a backing at least 10 cm (4 in) wider and longer than the quilt top.

Wadding (batting): 105 x 105 cm (41⅜ x 41⅜ in), or at least 5 cm (2 in) wider and longer than the quilt top.

Sewing thread: Strong sewing thread in matching or contrasting colour to the fabric.

Quilting thread: 10 g ball of pearl cotton crochet thread size 8 or similar in colour of your choice.

TOOLS AND EQUIPMENT

Freezer paper
Paper scissors
Quilter's rule
Tailor's chalk, fabric marker or quilter's crease
Fabric scissors
Rotary cutter and cutting mat
Sewing machine
Sewing needles and quilting needles
Iron and ironing board

CUTTING OUT THE BLOCKS

Using a quilter's rule, mark out 16 fabric blocks each measuring 24 x 24 cm (9½ x 9½ in). If you are making the entire quilt yourself, you can draw the squares onto larger lengths of fabric to provide a guideline to work within. Once you have completed the appliqué, you can then trim the blocks to size before piecing. If several people are contributing blocks for the quilt, cut out all the fabric squares first so that they can be worked on simultaneously by many hands.

MAKING AND ATTACHING THE APPLIQUÉ SHAPES

One — Draw a selection of geometric or organic shapes on to the matt side of the freezer paper. You can either draw the shapes freehand or use a ruler or trace around objects. Cut out the paper shapes. I chose simple organic shapes, with some blocks having a single larger shape while other blocks had a collection of smaller shapes.

Two — Choose which fabric you are using for each of the different shapes. Following the instructions on pages 66–67, make up the appliqué pieces. Remember to clip into any curves so that the fabric sits flat and the curves are smooth.

Three — Decide which appliqué shapes you want to apply to each block. When you are happy with the composition, tack (baste) (see page 40) all of the appliqué shapes in place to prevent them moving around.

Four — Following the instructions on page 68, sew the appliqué shapes to the blocks using invisible stitching.

ASSEMBLING THE QUILT TOP

One — Cut out the individual blocks along the guidelines if still in a larger piece of fabric. If necessary, trim the edges of each block to neaten and make sure they are level and square.

Two — Arrange the blocks into four rows of four, making sure none of the same colours are touching and that the same colour combinations are not too close to each other. Play with the direction of the shapes as well as the colour placement to create an informal design.

Three — Once you are happy with the composition, sew the blocks into rows and then the rows into the quilt top with a 1-cm (⅜-in) seam allowance, taking care to line up the vertical and horizontal seams across all the strips. Turn the quilt top over and give it a final press to neaten.

CONSTRUCTING AND FINISHING THE QUILT

One   Construct the quilt by assembling the layers (see pages 38–41).

Two   Quilt the quilt top in any way that you like and using quilting stitches (see pages 30 and 34–35). I quilted simple straight lines spaced 1.25 cm (½ in) apart to create a close stitch pattern for added texture and to let the appliquéd shapes stand out, but you could follow the lines of your shapes or quilt each shape individually to create a different effect.

Three   Self-bind the edges of the quilt following the instructions on page 51.

Tip   The way this quilt is constructed, with 16 equal-sized blocks pieced together to make up the quilt top, it lends itself perfectly to being a group project. Or if you are making the entire quilt yourself, you can slowly build up the design whenever you have time. It is also a convenient way to make a larger quilt when you are short on space

---

SKIMMING STONES CUSHION

The organic shapes scattered across the surface of the Skimming Stones Cushion are reminiscent of the rocks and stones of Cornish beaches. The appliqué pattern is inspired by my childhood outings to the coast of Cornwall, collecting and skimming stones from the shoreline, but you may be inspired by your own collection of objects gathered on a nature walk.

Size: 55 x 55 cm (21½ x 21½ in).

MATERIALS

Cushion front and envelope back: 60 cm (23½ in) of 138-cm (54-in) wide medium-weight cotton or linen.

Backing fabric for the quilted cushion front: 66 x 66cm (26 x 26 in) of lightweight cotton or linen such as cotton lawn.

Appliqué: Selection of scraps or remnants of cotton or linen in different colours.

Wadding (batting): 61 x 61 cm (24 x 24 in) square.

Binding: At least 3 m (3¼ yd) of 7.5-cm (3-in) wide straight binding in a contrasting colour to the cushion (see pages 42–49).

Sewing thread: Strong sewing thread to match your chosen fabric.

Quilting thread: 10 g ball of pearl cotton crochet thread size 8 or similar in colour of your choice.

55 x 55 cm (22 x 22 in) square cushion pad.

TOOLS AND EQUIPMENT

Metre ruler (yardstick) or quilter's rule
Tailor's chalk, fabric marker or quilter's crease
Fabric scissors
Rotary cutter and cutting mat
Freezer paper
Sewing machine
Sewing needles and quilting needles
Iron and ironing board

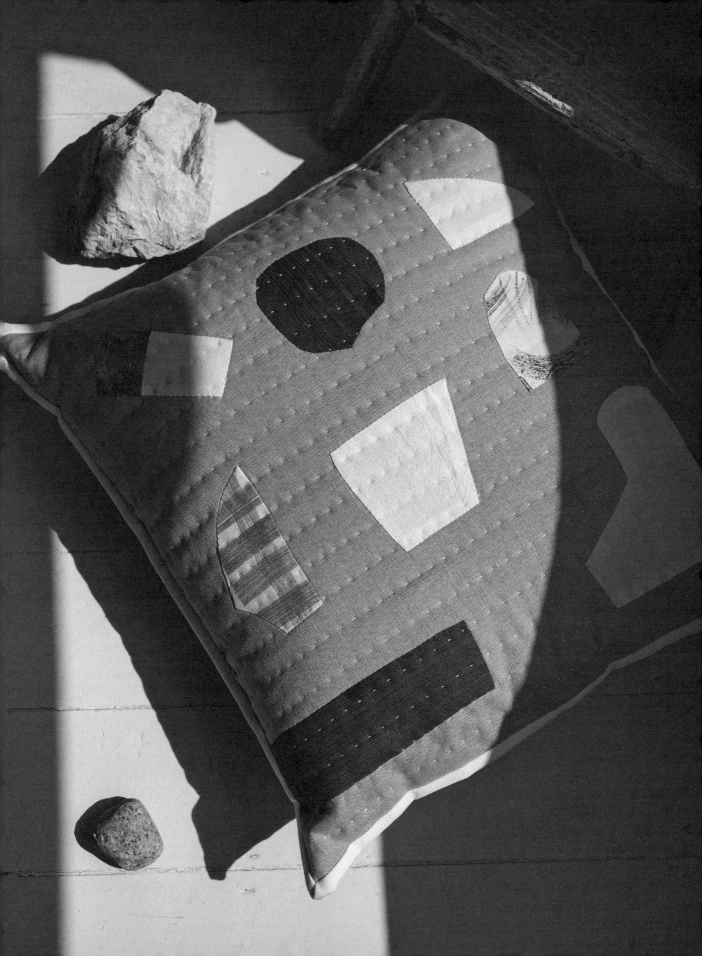

CUTTING THE CUSHION FRONT AND BACKS

From the cotton or linen fabric, cut the following pieces:

Cushion front – one 56 x 56-cm (22 x 22-in) square
Cushion backs – two 56 x 36-cm (22 x 14¼-in) rectangles

MAKING THE QUILTED CUSHION FRONT

One   Press the backing fabric for the quilted cushion front (not the fabric for the envelope cushion back).

Two   Tape the pressed backing fabric to your work surface and centre the wadding (batting) on top. Lay the cushion front over the wadding with the right side facing upwards. Keep the edges of all the layers straight and even, checking with a ruler if necessary.

Three   Tack (baste) the cushion front pieces together around the edges, working through all the layers (see page 40).

MAKING AND ATTACHING THE APPLIQUÉ SHAPES

One   Draw a selection of organic shapes on to the matt side of the freezer paper. You can either draw the shapes freehand or use a ruler or trace around objects. Cut out the paper shapes. I chose simple organic shapes based on the rocks and stones of the beaches of my childhood.

Two   Choose which fabric you are using for each of the different shapes. Following the instructions on pages 66–67, make up the appliqué pieces. Remember to clip into any curves so that the fabric sits flat and the curves are smooth.

Three   Arrange the appliqué shapes on the cushion front. When you are happy with the composition, tack (baste) all of the appliqué shapes in place to prevent them from moving around.

Four   Following the instructions on page 68, sew the appliqué shapes to the cushion front using invisible stitching.

QUILTING AND CONSTRUCTING THE CUSHION

One

Quilt the cushion front in any way that you prefer and using quilting stitches (see pages 30 and 34–35). I stitched simple straight lines spaced 2.5 cm (1 in) apart across the entire cushion front to create a close stitch pattern for added texture and to let the appliquéd shapes stand out, but you could follow the lines of your shapes or quilt each shape individually to create a different effect. Begin and end the quilting stitches within the seam allowance. Trim away any excess wadding (batting) and backing.

Two

To make the cushion back and construct the cushion, including binding the edges, follow the instructions on pages 137–138.

Tip

Freezer paper has a matt side and a shiny side. The matt side is the side on which you draw the shapes that you want to appliqué. The shiny side is the side that sticks to the fabric when run over with a hot iron. The freezer paper template can be pressed onto the right side of the fabric, in which case you should draw the shape to the exact size required with no seam allowance added and do not reverse. But if you choose to adhere the freezer paper to the wrong side of the fabric, then you will need to draw your shape in reverse.

DAY POUCH

This simple and practical pouch is great for carrying those essential items you might need day-to-day. Created from small curved patchwork blocks, you can personalise your pouch by using different fabrics and rearranging the blocks to create interesting patterns. The pouch is self-lined and has a zip fastener (zipper) to keep your items safe and secure.

Size: 25 x 20 cm (9¾ x 8 in).

MATERIALS

Outer pouch and binding: 40 cm (15¾ in) of 150-cm (59-in) or 114-cm (45-in) wide medium-weight cotton or linen in each of two different colours.

Backing/lining: 45 x 30 cm (17¾ x 12 in) of cotton or linen, or at least 10 cm (4 in) wider and longer than the outer pouch.

Wadding (batting): Approx. 40 x 25 cm (15¾ x 10 in), or at least 5 cm (2 in) wider and longer than the outer pouch.

Sewing thread: Strong sewing thread to match your chosen fabric.

Quilting thread: 10 g ball of pearl cotton crochet thread size 8 or similar in colour of your choice.

Paper for templates: 35 x 35 cm (13¾ x 13¾ in) piece of dot-and-cross pattern paper or brown parcel paper.

26-cm (10-in) closed-end zip fastener (zipper).

TOOLS AND EQUIPMENT

Metre ruler (yardstick) and pencil
Paper scissors
Quilter's rule
Tailor's chalk, fabric marker or quilter's crease
Fabric scissors
Rotary cutter and cutting mat
Sewing machine
Sewing needles and quilting needles
Iron and ironing board

MAKING THE TEMPLATES

The pouch is formed of 12 quarter-circle blocks, each with a finished size of 12 x 12 cm (4¾ x 4¾ in). Three blocks are stitched together in rows and then the four rows are joined to create the quilted outer pouch, lining up the seams as you go. To make the template for the pouch outer, draw a 35 x 20-cm (13¾ x 8-in) rectangle on your paper. Measure and mark the points 4 cm (1⅝ in) in from either side along the top edge. Using a ruler, draw a sloping line down and outwards from the marked point to the corresponding corner below. Cut out the template. To make the template for the patchwork block, draw a 12 x 12-cm (4¾ x 4¾-in) square on your paper. Cut out the template. This template will be used later to trim the blocks to size after they have been pieced together. (Some fabric will be lost in the curved seams.)

MAKING THE PATCHWORK OUTER POUCH

One — Cut out six 15 x 15-cm (6 x 6-in) squares from each colour fabric, giving you a total of 12 squares.

Two — With right sides facing upwards, layer two squares in different colours on top of each other on the cutting mat. Using the rotary cutter, firmly cut a quarter-circle shape freehand through both layers in one corner. Repeat with all the remaining squares.

Three — Separate the blocks and pair each quarter-circle shape with a contrast-colour border. Fit the quarter-circles into place on both panels with curved edges touching. To join the first panel, place the quarter-circle and border with right sides together and pin together all along the curve. With the quarter-circle on the bottom and the border on the top, stitch the two pieces together around the curve with a 0.5-cm (¼-in) seam allowance. To avoid puckers, work slowly and make sure the curved seam sits evenly. Check which side the seam naturally wants to curve towards and press it to that side. Turn the panel over and press it again to smooth out the seam.

Four — Place the panel on the cutting mat with the template on top, lining it up so that the apex of the curve sits within the middle of the template – you don't want to cut off the top of the curve or lose it in a seam. Trim around the template with the rotary cutter to create a neat 12 x 12-cm (4¾ x 4¾-in) block. Repeat until you have 12 blocks, pieced and trimmed.

Five — Arrange the blocks into three rows of four. Once you are happy with the composition, sew the blocks into rows and then the rows into the patchwork outer pouch with a 1-cm (⅜-in) seam allowance, taking care to line up the vertical and horizontal seams across all the strips. Turn the patchwork outer pouch over and give it a final press.

When arranging the patchwork blocks, you can either alternate the direction of your curves, or have them matching and all facing in the same direction.

QUILTING THE POUCH

One
With wrong sides together, fold the patchwork in half widthways along the seam between the second and third rows. With the right side facing outwards and the folded edge nearest to you, lay the folded patchwork on the cutting mat.

Two
Pin the pouch outer template to the patchwork, placing the longest edge of the template along the fold. Using a rotary cutter and cutting mat, trim around the side and top edges of the template but do not cut along the folded edge nearest to you. Unfold the patchwork piece and lay it out flat. To stop the stitching from unravelling and to stabilise the patchwork, sew a line of machine stitching 0.5 cm (¼ in) inside the outer edges.

Three
With the right side facing downwards, lay the backing/lining flat on your work surface. Place the wadding (batting) on top. Now lay the patchwork outer bag over the wadding (batting) with right side facing upwards. Tack (baste) the layers together with long stitches (see pages 38–40).

Four
Stitch with quilting stitches (see pages 30 and 34–35) as preferred. I worked straight lines of quilting stitches at 2.5-cm (1-in) intervals that run from the opening down the pouch and back up to the other side of the opening. Trim the backing/lining and wadding (batting) to the same size as the patchwork outer pouch.

CONSTRUCTING THE POUCH

One
With the right sides of the pouch outer together, re-fold the quilted pouch outer in half along the central seam, aligning the sloping edges. Join the pouch outer along the sloping edges with a 1-cm (⅜-in) seam allowance.

Two
From the remaining fabric used for the patchwork in your preferred colour, cut three strips to use as binding for the pouch. One should measure 60 x 4.5 cm (23½ x 1¾ in) and the other two should measure 25 x 4.5 cm (9¾ x 1¾ in). Either make these three strips as individual pieces or make one long strip measuring at least 110 cm (42¾ in) and cut it into smaller sections.

Three	Take one of the 25-cm (9¾-in) lengths of binding and press one short end over to the wrong side by 1 cm (⅜ in). With the right side of the binding together with the right side of the lining of the pouch, place the binding along the sloping seam of the pouch with raw edges aligned and so that the folded end of the binding is in line with the bottom fold of the pouch. Stitch the binding in place with a 1-cm (⅜-in) seam allowance.
Four	Fold the unstitched edge of the binding back, then press. Next, fold the binding over the sloping edge of the pouch. Press 1 cm (⅜ in) under along the unstitched edge of the binding and either hand stitch the binding in place or topstitch using your sewing machine. Repeat steps 3–4 with the second 25-cm (9¾-in) length of binding on the opposite seam.
Five	Flatten one of the bound side seams so it lies directly over the bottom fold. This will create a triangle, with the side seam running through the middle. Measure 4 cm (1⅝ in) down from the tip of the triangle and mark a horizontal line across the corner. Machine stitch along the marked line, backstitching at the start and finish to secure the stitching. This is a slightly bulkier part of the pouch, so use a heavier weight needle in the machine and take it slowly. The box seam created will give the pouch a flat bottom.

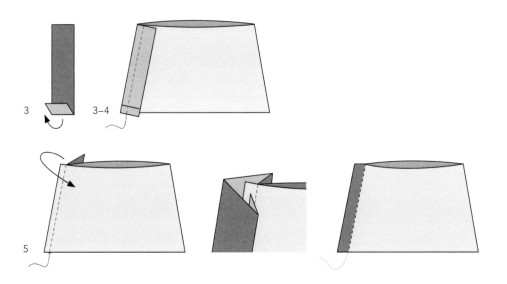

Six	With the pouch still inside out, pin the longest binding strip around the opening, leaving 5 cm (2 in) of excess binding free at the start. Stitch the binding with a 1-cm (⅜-in) seam all the way around the opening, stopping 10 cm (4 in) from the end.
Seven	Take the two loose tails of binding to the point of the pouch opening where they meet, pin them together at the meeting point and then stitch the ends together following the instructions on page 47. Trim away any excess binding and press open the seam. Stitch the remaining binding down – it should sit perfectly in the gap.
Eight	Fold the unstitched edge of the binding back and across the opening, then press. Next, fold the binding over the opening to the right side of the pouch to enclose the raw edge. Turn the pouch right side out. Press 1 cm (⅜ in) under along the unstitched edge of the binding and hand stitch the binding in place using blind stitch (see page 35).

ADDING THE ZIP FASTENER (ZIPPER)

One	Open up the zip fastener (zipper). Using the binding as a guide, pin one side of the zip tape to the inside of the opening, positioning the first 3–4 cm (1¼–1⅝ in) of the zip tape along the side seam so that the closed end of the zip sits at the very beginning of the opening. At the opposite end of the opening, tuck any excess zip tape down inside the pouch along the side seam. Repeat to attach the second side of the zip tape.
Two	Hand stitch the zip fastener (zipper) in place with small neat running stitches, catching only the lining of the pouch and not going through to the front. Stitch from seam to seam on each side, starting from the open end of the zip.
Three	The excess zip tape and zip pull are still folded down inside the pouch. Wiggle the zip pull up to the opening so you can easily open and close your pouch.

BUCKET TOTE BAG

The Bucket Tote Bag is a roomy and practical bag to use while out and about. The round bucket design lends itself to being quilted and can be made using many of the workshop techniques in this book. For this project I have used a selection of navy and black cotton and linen remnants to create an informal patchwork composition, and added a handy deep front pocket for essentials.

Size: 39 x 25 cm (15 x 10 in) excluding strap.

MATERIALS

Outer bag: Selection of scraps or remnants of cotton or linen pieced together to make an 81 x 42-cm (32 x 16½-in) patchwork block.

Bag base, lining, handles and pocket: 60 cm (22¾ in) of 150-cm (59-in) wide medium-weight cotton or linen.

Wadding (batting): Approx. 86 x 47 cm (34 x 18½ in), or at least 5 cm (2 in) wider and longer than the outer bag.

Sewing thread: Strong sewing thread to match your chosen fabric.

Quilting thread: 10 g ball of pearl cotton crochet thread size 8 or similar in colour of your choice.

Paper for templates: 120 x 60 cm (47¼ x 23¾ in) piece of dot-and-cross pattern paper or brown parcel paper.

TOOLS AND EQUIPMENT

Metre ruler (yardstick) and pencil
Paper scissors
Quilter's rule
Tailor's chalk, fabric marker or quilter's crease
Fabric scissors
Rotary cutter and cutting mat
Sewing machine
Sewing needles and quilting needles
Iron and ironing board

MAKING THE TEMPLATES

To make the template for the bag and lining sides, draw a 81 x 42-cm (32 x 16½-in) rectangle on your paper. Cut out the template, fold it in half lengthwise, then mark the centre point along each long side. To make the template for the bag and lining base, draw a circle with a 27-cm (10½-in) diameter using a pair of compasses or by tracing around a small plate or bowl.

MAKING THE PATCHWORK OUTER BAG

One — Using any of the techniques outlined in Workshop Three (see pages 54–63), join your selection of fabrics into a patchwork block measuring slightly larger than the 81 x 42-cm (32 x 16½-in) template. Play around with the composition and colours as you grow your block. Press all the seams open.

Two — Pin the rectangular template to the patchwork. Using a rotary cutter and cutting mat, trim around the template to neaten the edges. To stop the stitching from unravelling and to stabilise the patchwork, sew a line of machine stitching 0.5 cm (¼ in) inside the outer edges. Using the templates, cut out two circles, one pocket and one rectangular bag lining from the lining fabric.

Three — Lay the wadding (batting) flat, centre the patchwork on top with right side facing upwards, then tack (baste) together to secure (see pages 38–40).

Four — Stitch the patchwork and wadding (batting) with quilting stitches (see pages 30 and 34–35) as preferred. Begin the stitching 1 cm (⅜ in) inside the edges so the stitches are not cut when making up the bag. For my bag, I quilted within the large patchwork pieces in different directions to add interest to the quilted surface, working the stitch lines roughly 1 cm (⅜ in) apart. Trim the wadding (batting) back to the size of the patchwork.

ADDING THE POCKET

One Press a 1.5-cm (⅝-in) double hem along one long straight edge of the pocket piece, making sure the raw edge is hidden inside the folds. Using your sewing machine, topstitch along the hem.

Two Press a 1.5-cm (⅝-in) hem along each of the remaining three edges.

Three Fold the quilted outer bag in half both lengthways and widthways to find and mark the centre point. Do the same with the hemmed pocket piece, again marking the centre point. Matching up the centre points, place the pocket with right side facing upwards over the quilted outer bag with the double-hemmed edge at the top. Top stitch the pocket in place along the sides and bottom, leaving the top edge open.

CONSTRUCTING THE OUTER BAG

One With right sides together, fold the quilted outer bag in half lengthways. Mark the centre point on the fold along the bottom edge, then join the two short sides with a 1-cm (⅜-in) seam allowance. Press the seam open.

Two Match up the side seam with the marked point on the opposite side of the patchwork piece. Mark the two new folds at the sides, again on the bottom edge. These marks will be used later to line up the bag base and sides.

Three For the bag base, fold one circle of lining fabric in half and then in half again. Mark the point of all four folds.

Four With right sides together, match the marks on the bag base with those on the outer bag and pin in place. Insert more pins all the way around the base to ensure a perfect fit. Sew around the base with a 1-cm (⅜-in) seam allowance, making sure the fabric doesn't pucker. Turn the bag outer right side out and steam gently to press the seam.

MAKING THE HANDLES

One   Fold and stitch each handle piece following steps 1–2 of Making the strap on page 95.

Two   Trim the ends of each strap to straighten. Arrange the bag outer so that the seam is in the centre of one side. Place one end of the first handle between the centre seam and the side edge, aligning the straight end with the top edge of the bag outer, then pin in place. Run the strap across to the other side of the centre seam and position the other end to match the first end, making sure the handle is evenly spaced and not twisted. Repeat with the second handle on the opposite side of the bag to match the first. The handles should be running downwards to the base of the bag and laying flat.

MAKING THE LINING

One   Make the bag lining following steps 1–4 on page 175, but leaving a 12-cm (4¾-in) gap in the side seam that will be used later to turn the bag right side out once lined. Leave the lining wrong side out.

CONSTRUCTING THE BAG

One   With right sides together, slide the bag outer inside the lining. The handles must sit between the bag outer and lining. Align the top edges and side seams, then stitch all the way around the opening with a 1-cm (⅜-in) seam allowance. Make sure the ends of the handles are stitched in the seam.

Two   Pull the bag and handles through the gap in the lining so the bag is now right side out, the lining sits inside the bag and seam is hidden. Press all the edges.

Three   Using matching thread, hand sew the gap in the lining closed with slip stitch (see page 35).

Tip   You can make lots of variations of this bag using different patchwork patterns and appliqué techniques from the workshops. You can create it with or without pockets, or place the pocket on the lining instead of the outside. Make the bag personal to you by trying out different combinations.

LANDSCAPE QUILT

Fabric can be used to paint a picture, building up layers within a composition and abstracting shapes to depict a scene. The Landscape Quilt is inspired by photographs that my father has taken of the Cornish countryside. You can use any photos personal to you in order to create your own design using the same technique.

Size: 140 x 140 cm (55 x 55 in).

MATERIALS

Quilt top base: 140 x 140 cm (55 x 55 in) cotton or linen, or piece together smaller sections of fabric to create a base the size needed for the quilt top. (I joined two long lengths to create the base for my quilt top.)

Appliqué: Selection of scraps or remnants of cotton or linen in different colours.

Backing: 150 x 150 cm (59 x 59 in) of cotton or linen, or piece together smaller sections of fabric to create a backing at least 10 cm (4 in) wider and longer than the quilt top.

Wadding (batting): 145 x 145 cm (57 x 57 in), or at least 5 cm (2 in) wider and longer than the quilt top.

Binding: At least 620 cm (245 in) of 10-cm (4-in) wide straight binding.

Sewing thread: Strong sewing thread to match your chosen fabric.

Quilting thread: 10 g ball of pearl cotton crochet thread size 8 or similar in colour of your choice.

Paper to create your design.

TOOLS AND EQUIPMENT

Metre ruler (yardstick) and pencil
Freezer paper (optional)
Paper scissors
Quilter's rule
Tailor's chalk, fabric marker or quilter's crease
Fabric scissors
Rotary cutter and cutting mat
Sewing machine
Sewing needles and quilting needles
Iron and ironing board

QUILT PLAN

Referring to your chosen image for inspiration, sketch out a plan for your quilt design on paper. I worked from photographs of the Cornish landscape taken by my father. Pick out the key shapes from the image and reduce them down to their simplest forms. Do not add any fine detail, simply block out the forms to transform the original landscape image into a series of abstract shapes. Cut out the individual shapes to make templates for the appliqué pieces. Move the templates around, playing with the scale by redrawing the shapes if preferred, and layering them over one another.

When making any simple quilted piece that incorporates appliqué, I prefer to construct the layers – but not quilt them – before adding the appliquéd shapes. I find this provides a more stable backing on which to sew when applying the appliqué. It also means that you can rework the design multiple times by arranging and re-arranging the appliqué shapes on the background until you are happy with the composition, so that you can see the design come together.

CONSTRUCTING THE QUILT TOP

One
If you are making the quilt top base from a single length of fabric, cut it to 140 x 140 cm (55 x 55 in) or your preferred size. If you are piecing together two or more sections to make the base, follow the instructions on pages 54–63 to join them into a patchwork the size required.

Two
Following the instructions on page 38–40, making sure that all edges are straight and even, layer the backing fabric, wadding (batting) and quilt top on top of each other, centering each piece and ensuring that there is an even border of backing fabric around each edge. Tack (baste) all of the layers together.

MAKING AND ATTACHING THE APPLIQUÉ SHAPES

One — Referring to your composition, identify which shapes are in the background, the middle ground and the foreground. Starting with the shapes in the background of your design, find a fabric scrap for the appliqué that are roughly the same size as the drawn shape. Place the fabric scrap right side facing upwards in position on the quilt top base and tack it in place by making a few large stitches in the centre. Rather than sewing neatly around the edges, you just need to secure the fabric temporarily to the base.

Two — Using fabric scissors, trim the edges of the fabric scrap into the desired shape but with an additional 1-cm (⅜-in) border all the way around. If you want to replicate faithfully your drawn shape, use a fabric marker to trace around the paper template to give a guideline for cutting. I prefer not to overthink the process or worry about being too neat and cut the fabric freehand without a guideline. In terms of painting, I think of it as getting the base colour down.

Three — Fold under the edges of the roughly cut shape, pressing them as you work around the appliqué piece. You can further adjust the shape by manipulating the edges of the appliqué piece as you fold and press to refine the shape.

Four — Using blind stitch (see page 35), stitch the appliqué piece to the quilt top base all the way around the outside edge. If your appliqué piece overhangs an outer edge of the base, simply stitch down the edges of the appliqué piece that falls within the base.

Five — Repeat steps 1–4 for all the remaining appliqué pieces that make up the background layer of your composition.

Six — Referring again to your composition, identify those shapes that make up the middle ground. Using another selection of fabric scraps, repeat steps 1–4 to build up the next layer of appliqué shapes.

Seven — To complete your design, repeat steps 1–4 for the remaining foreground shapes of your composition.

Tip — Bear in mind the weight of the fabrics that you are using for the appliqué pieces. Using lots of thick fabrics will make it more difficult to stitch through all the layers when you are quilting the project. I recommend using lightweight fabrics if you are building up multiple layers. I find that three layers is the maximum number before it gets too difficult to stitch.

CONSTRUCTING AND FINISHING THE QUILT

One   Quilt the quilt top in any way that you like and using one of the quilting stitches (see pages 30 and 34–35). If your design is busy, consider working your quilting stitches in straight lines so as not to distract from any complex shapes. Alternatively, use the appliqué shapes as a guide for the quilting stitches and follow the outlines of the pieces to add emphasis to the design.

Two   Bind the edges of the quilt with the pre-prepared binding strip, attaching the binding to the back of the quilt first with a 1-cm (⅜ -in) seam allowance before pressing the binding to the front of the quilt to create a wide frame of binding around the outer edge of the quilt (see pages 42–49). Finish the binding by hand. At 10 cm (4 in) wide, the binding used on this quilt is wider than the standard width used for the other projects in this book.

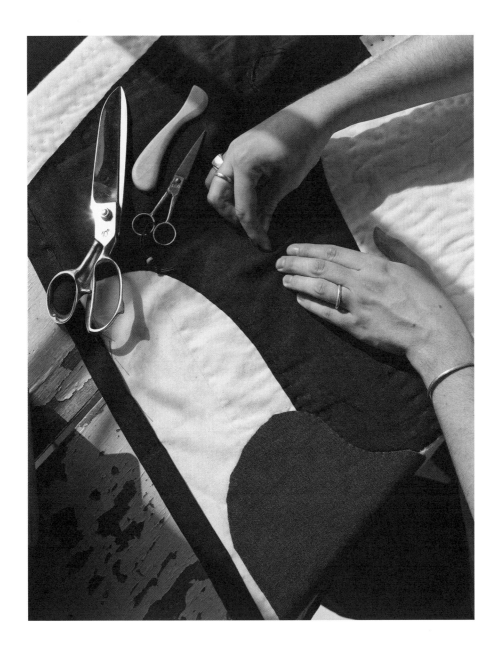

INDEX

Quilting projects are in *italics*

A

Abstract Quilt 84–9
activism and quilting 12
African/African American
      quilting 11
AIDS Memorial Quilt 12
Alabama: Gee's Bend
      quilters 11
American quilting 11
Amish quilting 11
appliqué 65–9
      attaching 68
      turned-edge appliqué 66–7

B

Baban Quilt 154–9
backing layer 38
      self-binding 51
bags
      Bucket Tote Bag 172–7
      Day Pouch 166–71
      Festival Pouch 114–19
      Forager Bag 90–5
      Wheat Bag 146–9
Bangladesh 12
basting 40–1
batting 20, 38
beeswax 17

Bengal 12
binding 42–51
      attaching 43
      hand-finishing 48
      joining 46–7
      making your own 42–3
      self-binding 51
      twofold binding 42–9
blind stitch 35, 68
boro mending 12
Broken Ladder Quilt 96–101
Bucket Tote Bag 172–7

C

care of quilts 23
chalk 17
Circular Cushion 102–7
collages: *Textile Collage* 130–3
colour 23
Colour Block Quilt 74–7
construction 37–51
      binding 42–51
      layering 38–41
      quilting 41
cotton 20
creasing 16
curved patchwork 57–61
cushions
      Circular Cushion 102–7
      Moor Stone Cushion 134–9

Rituals Cushion 140–5
Skimming Stones Cushion
      160–5
cutters 16
cutting mats 16

D

Day Pouch 166–71
dyeing 20

E

England 11
equipment 16–19

F

fabric markers 16, 17, 41
fabrics 9, 20
Festival Pouch 114–19
finishing the stitching 33
Forager Bag 90–5
free-form patchwork 54–5
freezer paper 17, 66

G

Gee's Bend quilters 11

RESOURCES

Ada & Ina
Linen textiles
https://www.linenfabrics.co.uk/

Merchant & Mills
Textiles and haberdashery
https://merchantandmills.com/

Mono Antiques
Antique and vintage Japanese textiles
https://www.etsy.com/uk/shop/MonoAntiques

Offset Warehouse
Eco and sustainable fabrics
https://www.offsetwarehouse.com

Organic Textile Company
Organic and Fairtrade fabrics
https://organiccotton.biz/

Ray Stitch
Textiles, haberdashery and quilting supplies
https://www.raystitch.co.uk/

The New Craft House
Designer, deadstock fabrics
https://shop.thenewcrafthouse.com/

The Sewing Retreat
Organic textiles and threads
https://www.thesewingretreat.co.uk/

Truro Fabrics
Textiles, haberdashery and quilting supplies
https://www.trurofabrics.com/

ACKNOWLEDGEMENTS

I would like to dedicate this book to the people in my life who have believed in me, stood by me and allowed me to be myself. Since childhood and throughout my adult life, making and creating has been so important to me and your kind words, mentorship and encouragement will always be remembered. Thank you.

To my mother, father and sister, this book is inspired by you. A childhood full of memories brought this book to life, and I am so thankful for that. Your encouragement and support have meant so much over the years and I can't thank you enough. From skimming stones, collecting shells and making potions, this book is an ode to you and the inspiration you are, and will always be.

To my extended family, Gran and Grandad A, a lifetime of stories and family memories inspire me every day and I think of you often whilst quilting and sewing. You are part of this book in so many ways.

To my Nan and Grandad (with the pigeons) who were always so giving, you are not here to share this moment with me and we all miss you so much.

To my friends who have helped me sew, iron, quilt, set up stools, driven me to events, taken photos, been in photos, listened to me go on about anything to do with sewing and making, put me up for weeks at a time to attend trade fairs, you know who you are and you mean the world to me, thank you.

A special thank you to Jane Briscoe who helped sew and quilt some of the projects in this book. Without you this would have been impossible. You are a sewing queen and your support and friendship means the world to me.

To Danny, I could not have done this without you. Thank you for your unconditional support and understanding and for always holding my hand, I love you very much.

To Rob, Francis and everyone at Truro Fabrics who took a chance on an eager young boy who wanted to learn. You are always in my memories and I am so grateful to you for taking me under your wing. A special thank you and remembrance to Annie for your kind words. I will never forget you.

To the community of makers and designers who I have had the pleasure of working with in recent years, to the stores, stockists and collaborators who have championed my work. You all have been an inspiration and guiding light on this journey. A big shout out to Alessandra, Ana, Phoebe, Charlotte and Fred who made my first trade show an incredible memory I will never forget.

To everyone who contributed or gifted materials used in this book; to my mum and her wonderful sourcing skills, and to Michelle and the Merchant & Mills team for your donation of beautiful textile remnants – your support is greatly appreciated.

Thank you to everyone at Hardie Grant Books, especially Kajal Mistry for discovering my work and for giving me the opportunity to create this book. Your confidence in me has meant so much and I will always be grateful to you.

Thank you to Louie Waller and Matt Russell. You understood my vision from the very beginning and through your beautiful styling and photography you brought my work to life in ways I could have only imagined. To Vanessa Masci, Marie Clayton and Kate Burkett who helped me make sense of my words and create a book to be so proud of. Thank you all for your patience and understanding – you turned my ideas into reality. Thank you.

ABOUT THE AUTHOR

Julius Arthur is a designer and maker residing in Sussex and founder of House of Quinn, a design studio with a considered approach to making handmade objects for living spaces. Working with renewed and consciously sourced textiles, his collections centre on using traditional techniques to create contemporary objects with a sense of place and function.

Published in 2021 by Hardie Grant Books

Hardie Grant Books (London)
5th & 6th Floors
52–54 Southwark Street
London SE1 1UN

hardiegrantbooks.com

British Library Cataloguing-in-Publication Data. A catalogue record for this book is available from the British Library.

Modern Quilting
ISBN: 9781784883942

10 9 8 7 6 5 4 3

Publisher and commissioner: Kajal Mistry
Project Editor: Kate Burkett
Design and Art Direction: Vanessa Masci
Illustrations: Vanessa Masci
Photographer: Matt Russell
Photography Assistants: Hannah Lemon and Matthew Hague
Prop Stylist: Louie Waller
Copy-editor: Marie Clayton
Proofreader: Lisa Pendreigh
Indexer: Cathy Heath
Production Controller: Nikolaus Ginelli

Colour reproduction by p2d
Printed and bound in China by C&C Offset Printing Co., Ltd.